Strategic Sport Communication

Authors Coombs and Harker provide step-by-step guidance on how the strategic communication process—an integration of marketing communication, public relations, and advertising—can be applied to sports communication for individual athletes, teams, and leagues.

The book is founded on the premise that the strategic communication process in sport communication is grounded in understanding the fans and sources of revenue. Looking at sports globally, it offers readers the traditional multi-step, linear approach to strategic communication message development along with the transmedia narrative transportation method, a non-linear approach that centers on narratives to engage target audiences and urge them to contribute their own material to messaging. With case studies and practical examples, it also highlights additional issues such as race and gender, social media, ethics, and athlete health.

It is an ideal text for undergraduate and graduate courses in public relations or strategic communication and sport communication.

An online instructor's manual accompanies the text, including lecture slides; a sample strategic sports communication plan; a test bank; links to key web sites that discuss sports and sports communication concerns; links to case studies with class discussion prompts; sample assignments; a sample course syllabus; and suggestions for further reading.

W. Timothy Coombs (Ph.D., Purdue University) is a full professor in the Department of Communication at Texas A&M University and holds the Abell Endowed Professorship in Liberal Arts. He was the 2002 recipient of the Jackson, Jackson & Wagner Behavioral Science Prize from the Public Relations Society of America and the 2013 Pathfinder Award from the Institute of Public Relations in recognition of his research contributions to the field and to the practice.

Jennifer L. Harker (Ph.D., The University of North Carolina at Chapel Hill) is an assistant professor of strategic communication in the Reed College of Media at West Virginia University. She researches sport communication, stakeholder perceptions, and media business models/product marketing.

Strategic Sport Communication

Traditional and Transmedia Strategies for a Global Sports Market

**W. Timothy Coombs
and Jennifer L. Harker**

Routledge
Taylor & Francis Group

NEW YORK AND LONDON

First published 2022
by Routledge
605 Third Avenue, New York, NY 10158

and by Routledge
2 Park Square, Milton Park, Abingdon, Oxon OX14 4RN

Routledge is an imprint of the Taylor & Francis Group, an informa business

© 2022 Taylor & Francis

Library of Congress Cataloging-in-Publication Data
Names: Coombs, W. Timothy, author. | Harker, Jennifer L., author.
Title: Strategic sport communication: traditional and transmedia strategies
for a global sports market / W. Timothy Coombs, Jennifer L. Harker.
Description: New York, NY : Routledge, [2022] |
Includes bibliographical references and index.
Identifiers: LCCN 2021012514 (print) | LCCN 2021012515 (ebook) |
ISBN 9780367902995 (hardback) | ISBN 9780367898724 (paperback) |
ISBN 9781003031161 (ebook)
Subjects: LCSH: Communication in sports. | Mass media and sports. |
Sports and globalization. | Sports–Marketing.
Classification: LCC GV567.5 .C68 2021082 (print) |
LCC GV567.5 (ebook) | DDC 070.4/49796–dc23
LC record available at https://lccn.loc.gov/2021012514
LC ebook record available at https://lccn.loc.gov/2021012515

ISBN: 978-0-367-90299-5 (hbk)
ISBN: 978-0-367-89872-4 (pbk)
ISBN: 978-1-003-03116-1 (ebk)

DOI: 10.4324/9781003031161

Typeset in Bembo
by Newgen Publishing UK

Access the Support Material: www.routledge.com/9780367898724

W. Timothy Coombs:
To Ash for his patience throughout this process.

Jennifer L. Harker:
I dedicate this accomplishment to my mother, Patricia Mary Chamberlin Treiber, who dedicated her entire life to loving and serving others.

Contents

About the Authors

W. Timothy Coombs (Ph.D. from Purdue University in Public Affairs and Issues Management) is a full professor in Department of Communication at Texas A&M University and holds the Abell Endowed Professorship in Liberal Arts. He has received the 2002 recipient of Jackson, Jackson & Wagner Behavioral Science Prize from the Public Relations Society of America and the 2013 Pathfinder Award from the Institute of Public Relations in recognition of his research contributions to the field and to the practice. He has won multiple PRIDE awards from the Public Relations Division of the National Communication Association for both books and research articles. He is also a member of the prestigious Arthur W. Page Society.

Dr. Coombs was a Fulbright Scholar in Estonia in the spring of 2013. In the fall of 2013 he was the named NEMO Professor at Lund University, Helsingborg Campus. In 2015 he was invited to lecture at Tsinghua University, Beijing. In 2015 he was designated an honorary professor in the Department of Business Communication at Aarhus University. He also has been editor of *Corporation Communication: An International Journal.*

Dr. Coombs' primary research focuses on crisis communication. In 1995, he published the first article that would lead to the articulation of the Situational Crisis Communication Theory (SCCT). SCCT is recognized as one of the most influential theories in crisis communication. His work has been at the forefront of establishing crisis communication as an identifiable research field within corporate communication. The recognition of his expertise is reflected in the variety of his speaking engagements in the U.S., Europe, and Asia. He has keynoted at a number of academic and practitioner conferences as well as lecturing on crisis communication at a number of international academic institutions. Since 2000, his works have been cited 6,300 times. Most of those citations involve the crisis communication research. His book *Ongoing Crisis Communication* has been cited over 3,700 times. His article summarizing SCCT on crisis communication in 2007 has been cited over 2,000 times. That article was awarded the 2014 Business Communication Impact Award from the Marshall School of Business at USC for being the most cited article over the past five years (2009–2013 in this case) in the top business communication journals.

Jennifer L. Harker (Ph.D., The University of North Carolina at Chapel Hill) is an assistant professor of strategic communication in the Reed College of Media at West Virginia University. She researches sport communication, stakeholder perceptions, and media business models/product marketing. In 2018, she developed an experiential learning program that is a course-based student-run advertising and public relations agency within the Reed College of Media. The agency has since won several American Advertising Awards and continues to service West Virginia-based clients across the state. She also teaches undergraduate media writing and market research courses. Before earning her doctorate and becoming a professor, Dr. Harker practiced across the media spectrum working in jobs from journalism to public relations and marketing, to corporate communication and sports promotion, in both for-profit and nonprofit business models. In addition to her graduate education as a Tar Heel, she earned an associate's degree in journalism at Amarillo College, a bachelor's degree in sociology at Arizona State University, and a master's degree in communication at West Texas A&M University.

Acknowledgments

W. Timothy Coombs: This book is due in part to my lifelong love of track and field, which was a result of running with friends starting in eighth grade. Running with them built great memories that I can relive when I run today.

Jennifer L. Harker: This textbook is a testament to mentorship. I am grateful to my coauthor, W. Timothy Coombs, for his leadership, guidance, and especially his faith and belief in me to accomplish this great task. I also wish to thank my gorgeous family for their unending support: David, Jordan, Brooklyn, Haven, and of course, our playful puppies Walnut and Peanut. You each make life grand.

Introduction

.

Sport communication is a rapidly growing area of study that covers a vast array of topics (see Chapters 1, 9, and 11). One of those topics that is seeing increased attention is how communication is used to help achieve the goals of various sports entities (teams, leagues, and individual athletes). While often appearing in public relations courses, the use of communication to achieve goals is knowns as strategic communication. The primary focus of *Strategic Sport Communication: Transmedia Campaign Strategies for a Global Sports Market* is to present a strategic communication view of sport communication. Strategic communication integrates marketing communication, public relations, and advertising to pursue specific organizational goals.

The five-step strategic communication process developed in the book (Chapters 4 through 8) can be applied to individual athletes, teams, and leagues. The strategic communication process in sport communication is grounded in an understanding of the fans (Chapter 3) and sources of revenue in sports (Chapter 2). The fans are a major factor in what make strategic communication unique in the sport communication context and revenue is critical business background information about sport. The key objectives are to understand how fans and revenue relate to strategic communication efforts in sport. The book does move beyond these two contextual factors to consider how additional issues, such as gender and athlete health (Chapters 10 and 11), can shape how sport communication messages are created and understood by target audiences.

The book first orients the reader to sport communication with an emphasis on fans, revenue generation, and role of strategic communication in sport communication. The next section unpacks the five-step strategic communication process. There is an additional section on transmedia storytelling and the transmedia narrative theory (TNT) approach to strategic communication (Chapter 9). The TNT approach centers on narratives to engage target audiences with the messages and urges targets to contribute their own material to the messaging. This is a newer approach that is less linear than the five-step process but well suited to sport communication because of the desire fans have to engage in sport. The last section considers crisis communication. Crises disrupt strategy and strategic communicators

DOI: 10.4324/9781003031161-1

must learn how to cope with such disruptions. Chapter 12 considers the basics of crisis communication and the unique aspects of managing crises in the sports context.

There are a number of important themes woven throughout this book including business goals, social media platforms, and the unique contextual aspects of sport that shape strategic sport communication. The book works to connect strategic communication to the business goals of sports organizations. Too often strategic communication, usually in the form of public relations, is presented separately from business goals creating a disconnect between the public relations messages and the larger goals of the organization. This book seeks to reinforce the need to merge business goals and strategic communication efforts.

The book provides a detailed understanding of how the digital environment and social media platforms are a natural part of modern strategic communication. Social media platforms are growing in use in sport communication because of the nature of fan communication. In the book, social media platforms are integrated into the fabric of how strategic communication is planned, executed, and evaluated. Transmedia storytelling is one of the ways social media platforms can change how people should approach strategic sport communication.

The book provides detailed discussion of the contextual factors for sport communication. Traditional sport communication textbooks explore intersecting topics such as gender, health, and technology in depth. Fan and fan behavior are core elements in appreciating the sport context. This book captures key ideas from the sport context and ties them to the strategic communication process in sport communication.

Objectives and Themes of the Book

1. To understand the value of a strategic communication approach to sport communication. (Sport communication as strategic communication)
2. To apply the five-step strategic communication process to the creation of sport communication messages. (Sport communication as strategic communication and nature of strategic communication)
3. To apply the TNT approach to the creation of sport communication messages. (An alternative approach to traditional strategic communication rooted in storytelling)
4. To appreciate the ways fans make strategic communication unique within the sports context. (Criticality of fans on sport communication)
5. To link strategic communication efforts to revenue generation. (Need to link strategic communication to organizational goals and monitor return on investment)

6. To appreciate and value the curating of fan content as part of sport communication (Role of social media platforms and fan generated content in strategic communication for sport)
7. To appreciate that sport communication occurs on different levels. (Sport communication involving individuals, teams, and leagues; this will include a recognition of special concerns for grassroots/community sports organizations)

1 Sport Communication, Strategic Communication, and Strategic Sport Communication

Defining Our Terms

You are about to learn more about strategic sport communication. The first step is to understand what the phrase strategic sport communication means. The phrase is a combination of very significant approaches to communication, sport communication and strategic communication. Moreover, these two areas of communication are very broad so it is helpful to begin the book by explaining sport communication, strategic communication, and the unique approach you get when melding the two into strategic sport communication.

Key Aspects of Sport Communication

Communicating about sport comes as naturally to some as talking about the weather. Sport offers us a way to connect to others. Moreover, sport communication represents a distinctive form of communication. Sport connects us to community, sport is entertainment, and sport even offers us a platform for social justice and helps our communities—through the entertainment of sport—to work toward cultural equalities. As professional communicators, sport is presented through myriad scholarly techniques. From critical cultural perspectives to sports media, sport is communicated globally in infinite ways. It is important to appreciate the complexity that is sport communication if you hope to engage in sport communication for a living.

Sport and Community

Sport *is* community. From pick-up soccer games at community fields to the grand stage of the Olympics, sport is rooted in community. Community is defined by *Webster's Dictionary* as "a feeling of fellowship with others." Sport connects people in countless ways. This book will present a number of facets regarding sport that should be considered when strategically communicating about sport, a sports entity or when communicating for a sports organization. But the only thing to keep in mind throughout your upcoming journey of creating a strategic sport communication campaign is the fact that any sport communication scholar will tell you: *in sport, communication norms*

DOI: 10.4324/9781003031161-2

are just incredibly different from virtually any other type or topic of communication. By the time you finish working through this textbook, you will come to understand why we assert such a claim.

Whether a sports fan or not, we regularly interact with one another through sport. Interactivity with one another through community and sport includes watching sports together, talking about sports together, playing sports together, attending sporting events together, and even cheering for a favorite team together. Interactivity through communication regarding sport is unique because sport can offer a universal, low-stakes opportunity to conversationally engage with others. For example, if a stranger on public transportation is wearing a hat with a team logo, it is easy to strike up conversation with that person about a recent game in which that team competed. Furthermore, when discussing sport, that same stranger-engaged conversation can even include a jab at that person's favorite team, especially if your favorite team is a rival of their favorite team. This type of discordant communication would not typically be extended to a stranger in good faith but, as we say: in sport, communication norms are different. Rivalry is actually a form of social support in sport communication (Harker, 2018). Typically, discordant communication is the antithesis to social support. Perhaps it is the nature of sports fans and their array of fan behavior, which we discuss in detail in Chapter 3, that sets this type of discord apart. Whatever it is, one might argue that discord is all part of the entertainment aspect of sport.

Sport as Entertainment

Sport is big business, as you will read in Chapter 2, but sport is also intertwined with every aspect of family and public life as a form of entertainment. We grow up competing in physical education classes and participating in little league, we attend or perform in Friday Night Lights in high school, and a major part of the college experience includes building identification with our institution through sport. Sport brings communities together through the entertainment it offers.

Sport as entertainment can be enjoyed as an active competitor within the sport or as a sport spectator. Either way, sport consumption involves sport communication. Sport is communicated to us visually, orally, textually, and even physically. Sport is spectacle. From the ancient days of the Roman Empire and the earliest creation of running, wrestling, boxing, or even jousting competitions, sport became spectacle by moving beyond competition and becoming entertainment. Today, we watch, discuss, read about, and participate in sport across the life span because sport as entertainment is cultivated within our cultures and enjoyed throughout our communities. People communicate about sport through online and offline social networks. We speak about sports with family and strangers, alike. And sport offers us infinite topics to discuss.

Sport and Social Justice

Sport offers a platform for social justice movements regarding a kaleidoscope of sociocultural matters because sport is all-inclusive, at least in interest and consumption. Sport is far from inclusive when we begin discussing race and gender, however; but because sport consumption is so intertwined with sport communication, sport offers a platform from which all interested parties can discuss these matters and utilize the grand stages of sport to spread messages for equality and equity as we all move forward together. More on social justice, as it relates to sports and culture, is included in Chapter 10. And in Chapter 11, we further this discussion by presenting the importance of athlete health and safety, and the conversations necessary for making sport safer and more inclusive, and how all of these sociocultural matters should remain at the forefront of strategic sport communication campaigns.

Common Perspectives for Sport Communication

Sport communication is researched and expressed from various "schools of thought" or perspectives. The two main perspectives are critical cultural studies and media studies. Critical cultural studies broadly includes race, gender, nationalism, and rhetoric. Media studies is a broad categorization that can include advertising, public relations, and journalism, to name a few. The differences between these two perspectives are slight but important. The ways in which these two perspectives are similar are 1) how we communicate and persuade regarding sport, and 2) how we present representation of and through sport in mass media. To explain, there are ten major areas of study in sport communication that can be categorized under either critical cultural studies or media studies and sometimes both. Those ten areas of sport communication include: 1) crisis, 2) gender, 3) industry, 4) marketing, 5) media, 6) nationalism, 7) mega-events, 8) race, 9) sport consumption, 10) all else (Hambrick, 2017). We communicate and provide perspective through critical cultural studies involving critical race theory, feminist theories, and rhetorical studies (Harker & Saffer, 2018). These perspectives include crisis, gender, nationalism, ability, and race, just to name a few. The media studies perspective on sport communication involves the framing and representation of all of those critical cultural matters, as well as the mass communication of the sports industry, and the promotion, marketing, consumption, and storytelling around sport. As you embark on your own campaign creation, you will no doubt come across these topical aspects of sport communication. It is important to keep in mind all the ways in which sport spans the psychological and sociological, which both perspectives convey. In Chapter 3 we discuss the psychological and sociological aspects of sport communication and in Chapter 5 we offer several qualitative and quantitative research methods that fall under both perspectives.

All combined, sport is communicated through community, as entertainment, for social justice and through various perspectives. To communicate professionally about sport, we must be thoughtful and strategic. In the next section we explain strategic communication and how sport communication and strategic communication come together as strategic sport communication.

Key Aspects of Strategic Communication

The previous section indicated how sport can be many things and how sport communication can be viewed from different perspectives. Sport communication can mean so many different things, which is why there are majors in sport communication. We are focusing on sport communication as it relates to strategic communication. Strategic communication refers to the purposeful use of communication by entities to help accomplish their goals (Frandsen & Johansen, 2017). In this section, we unpack why we choose to focus on sport communication as strategic communication.

We choose the term strategic communication to capture the array of purposive communication actions initiated by entities in sports. Public relations, advertising, and marketing communication are the three major forms of communication included in the strategic communication umbrella. Advertising tends to be the narrowest of the three. Advertising focuses on the use of paid channels (mass media and social media) to deliver messages that will create awareness of and interest in products and services. There is nonproduct advertising but that is a small part of advertising. Marketing communication reflects the promotion part of the four Ps of marketing. The other three Ps are price, product, and place. Promotion is about communicating with possible consumers about products and services. Both advertising and marketing focus primarily upon consumers and seek to sell products or services. Public relations seeks to build and to maintain relationships with a variety of stakeholders. While different from one another, these three communication functions do overlap with one another. A marketing communication effort might use both advertising and public relations. A public relations effort might use advertising. Integrated marketing communication (IMC) has argued for decades that we need to coordinate these communication functions (e.g., Manoli & Hodgkinson, 2020).

Sport Communication as Strategic Communication

Strategic communication is a perfect label to capture how sport communication is used to achieve organizational goals. Strategic communication can include not only advertising, public relations, and marketing communication, but corporate communication and organizational communication as well. So why should we view sport communication as strategic communication?

Strategic communication helps entities achieve their goals. Entities in sport would include individual athletes, teams, and leagues. All sport entities share two larger goals: 1) revenue generation and 2) favorable social evaluations. Sports entities, even those that are considered amateurs, need to generate revue to continue operations. Even college sports, which are nonprofit, need funding to play as do small, local sports entities such as Little League. Generating revenue is an essential goal for any sports entity. Favorable social evaluations attract people, including sponsors and fans, to sport entities. Social evaluation refers broadly to how stakeholders perceive the sports entity. Reputation is a form of social evaluation that most people are familiar with in some way. Reputation is a great example of how social evaluations have links to revenue generation. When you look at the valuation of a sports franchise, reputation is a major factor in determining how much a team is worth (Shea, 2018). Sports teams show a direct connection between social evaluations and revenue (Ertug & Castellucci, 2013).

Strategic communication has been used to increase revenue in organizations by increasing the demand for products and services. Strategic communication can be used to generate ticket and merchandise sales (da Silva & Las Casas, 2020). Social evaluations are heavily influenced by traditional and social media discussions of sports entities (Gill, 2018). Strategic communication has been used to influence both tradition media coverage and social media discussions of sports entities (e.g., Gibbs & Haynes, 2013; Sherwood, Nicholson, & Marjoribanks, 2017; Witkemper, Lim, & Wldburger, 2012). Hence, strategic communication can influence sport entity social evaluations, such as reputation, by generating favorable traditional and social media coverage of the sports entity.

Finally, strategic communication facilitates both revenue and social evaluation goals through fan cultivation. Fan cultivation includes recruiting new fans, retaining existing fans, and increasing fan social identification with a sports entity. Increased fan identification translates into both more positive reputations and revenue. As fans become more attached to a sports entity, they are developing more positive views of the sports entity (Money, Saraeva, Garnelo-Gomez, Pain, & Hillenbrand, 2017; Yousaf, Bashir, & Mishra, 2020). Fans have direct and indirect effects of revenue. As fan identification increases, so too does the purchasing of merchandise, including goods and services of sponsors and tickets (Kirkpatrick & Eason, 2019; Madrigal, 2000). Fan numbers help to attract sponsors and broadcast contracts. This includes both the number of fans at events and the number of fans active on social media (Kiani, Nazari, & Shabazpor, 2020). Strategic communication has proven especially useful at cultivating fans through social media engagement (Filo, Lock, & Karg, 2015). We should consider the strategic communication aspect of sport communication because strategic is integral to the success of sport entities—vital for achieving revenue generation and cultivating favorable social evaluations.

A message is the visible aspect of strategic communication. An example would be a tweet about season ticket plans. To create strategic communication efforts, you need to go through a process. Historically, the strategic communication process has been viewed as four steps: (1) researching, (2) planning, (3) communicating, and (4) evaluating (Van Ruler, 2015). We expand the strategic communication process to five steps by adding scanning and monitoring. Figure 1.1 illustrates the five-step strategic communication process. The old four-step model assumes you already have some idea of what you plan to do with the strategic communication efforts. Sport entities might have certain strategic communication activities that they conduct every year and the four-step model works fine. But how do you find possible new strategic communication efforts? Scanning and monitoring helps strategic communicators find opportunities and threats that could serve as the impetus for a strategic communication effort.

Research involves a variety of tools to discover more information about your communication situation. Findings threats and opportunities is only the beginning. It is important to understand a threat or opportunity before addressing either one. You must understand a situation before engaging in strategic communication if you hope to maximize the benefits from your strategic communication effort. Planning details what you hope to achieve with your strategic communication and how you hope to achieve this. Planning provides direction and guidance from your strategic communication and is informed by your research. Communicating is where you develop your messages and deliver them to your targets. Communicating involves how you structure the message, its visual elements, and the channels used to deliver the message to your targets. Evaluating is where you assess the effectiveness of your strategic communication effort. Evaluation allows you to show the value of a strategic communication effort as well as providing insights to help with future strategic communication efforts. Chapters 4 through 8 provides details about each of the five steps in the strategic communication process while Chapter 9 offers a transmedia-based approach to developing strategic communication efforts.

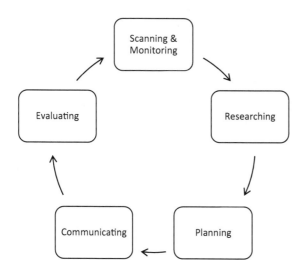

Figure 1.1 The strategic communication process.

Conclusion

Hopefully, you now have an appreciation of the broad areas of sport communication and strategic communication and what you get when you fuse the two to create strategic sport communication. Strategic sport communication is a specific way of approaching sport communication by treating it as a form of strategic communication. As this chapter suggests, there are myriad applications of both sport communication and strategic communication beyond strategic sport communication. But in this book, we are interested in developing the benefits of understanding sport communication through the lens of strategic communication—what we are calling strategic sport communication. When you reach the end of the book you will understand and be able to apply strategic sport communication to help solve problems and to leverage opportunities for various entities involved in sport.

References

da Silva, E. C., & Las Casas, A. L. (2020). Key elements of sports marketing activities for sports events. *International Journal of Business Administration, 11*(1), 11–21.

Ertug, G., & Castellucci, F. (2013). Getting what you need: How reputation and status affect team performance, hiring, and salaries in the NBA. *Academy of Management Journal, 56*(2), 407–431.

Filo, K., Lock, D., & Karg, A. (2015). Sport and social media research: A review. *Sport Management Review, 18*(2), 166–181.

Frandsen, F., & Johansen, W. (2017). Strategic communication. In C. Scott & L. Lewis (Eds.) *The international encyclopedia of organizational communication* (pp. 2250–2257). Malden, MA: John Wiley & Sons.

Gibbs, C., & Haynes, R. (2013). A phenomenological investigation into how Twitter has changed the nature of sport media relations. *International Journal of Sport Communication, 6*(4), 394–408.

Gill, R. (2018). The influence of media platforms on sport reputation: An Australian Football League case study. *Journal of Sports Media, 13*(1), 123–151.

Hambrick, M. E. (2017). Sport communication research: A social network analysis. *Sports Management Review, 20*(2), 170–183. doi:10.1016/j.smr.2016.08.002.

Harker, J. L. (2018). Crisis perceptions, fan behaviors, and egocentric discussion networks: An investigation into the impervious nature of NFL crises. Available from ProQuest Dissertations Publishing. Retrieved from https://search.proquest.com/openview/b8f6d30545a90ee15a5032c6cbb58706/1?pq-origsite¼gscholar&cbl¼18750&diss¼y

Harker, J. L., & Saffer, A. J. (2018). Mapping a subfield's sociology of science: A 25-year network and bibliometric analysis of the knowledge construction of sports crisis communication. *Journal of Sport and Social Issues, 42*, 369–392. doi:10.1177%2F0193723518790011

Kiani, M. S., Nazari, L., & Shabazpor, L. (2020). The impact of social media and the presence of fans at a sports event to attract private sector sponsors. *ACTIVE: Journal of Physical Education, Sport, Health and Recreation, 9*(2), 96–100.

Kirkpatrick, N., & Eason, C. (2019). The relationship between fan identification and collegiate athletic apparel brand preference. *Journal of Brand Strategy, 8*(2), 179–198.

Koronios, K., Psiloutsikou, M., Kriemadis, A., Zervoulakos, P., & Leivaditi, E. (2016). Sport sponsorship: The impact of sponsor image on purchase intention of fans. *Journal of Promotion Management, 22*(2), 238–250.

Madrigal, R. (2000). The influence of social alliances with sports teams on intentions to purchase corporate sponsors' products. *Journal of Advertising, 29*(4), 13–24.

Manoli, A. E., & Hodgkinson, I. R. (2020). The implementation of integrated marketing communication (IMC): evidence from professional football clubs in England. *Journal of Strategic Marketing, 28*(6), 542–563.

Money, K., Saraeva, A., Garnelo-Gomez, I., Pain, S., & Hillenbrand, C. (2017). Corporate reputation past and future: A review and integration of existing literature and a framework for future research. *Corporate Reputation Review, 20*(3–4), 193–211.

Shea, B. (2018, September 23). Why the Lions are worth less than most other NFL teams. *Crain's Detroit Business.* https://www.crainsdetroit.com/sports/why-lions-are-worth-less-most-other-nfl-teams

Sherwood, M., & Nicholson, M. (2017). Who controls sport news? Media relations and information subsidies in Australian sport media. *Media International Australia, 165*(1), 146–156.

Sherwood, M., Nicholson, M., & Marjoribanks, T. (2017). Access, agenda building and information subsidies: Media relations in professional sport. *International Review for the Sociology of Sport, 52*(8), 992–1007.

van Ruler, B. (2015). Agile public relations planning: The reflective communication scrum. *Public Relations Review, 41*(2), 187–194.

Witkemper, C., Lim, C. H., & Waldburger, A. (2012). Social media and sports marketing: Examining the motivations and constraints of Twitter users. *Sport Marketing Quarterly, 21*(3), 170–183.

Yousaf, A., Bashir, M., & Mishra, A. (2020). Revisiting spectator-based sports team reputation: strategic implications for team managers. *Corporate Reputation Review, 23*(1), 1–12.

2 Sport as an Industry

This chapter explains how sport is an industry and how the business side of sport operates. To be effective, strategic communicators must understand how a business operates and how strategic communication is utilized to achieve organizational goals. It is critical that strategic communicators understand how their actions can add value to the sport organization. This chapter reviews critical elements for understanding the business side of sport organizations. These critical elements shape how strategic communication can be used effectively in sport organizations—how strategic communication can help to achieve common sport organizational goals.

Sources of Revenue for Sport Organizations

The most valuable sports team in the world is the National Football League's Dallas Cowboys, which was worth $5 billion in 2019 (Badenhausen, 2020). Think for a moment about the last time you attended a sporting event, such as one in which the Dallas Cowboys compete. You purchased tickets; painstakingly balancing great seats with an affordable cost. On game day, you likely wore your team gear, perhaps a team jersey or t-shirt, or even a hat. You might have tailgated before the game began, and maybe even tuned into the pre-game show on television, the radio, or your ESPN app. Your ticket, which included a sponsor logo printed on it, was scanned as you entered the stadium. Inside the stadium, brands such as Pepsi or Bud Light were available for purchase as refreshments. The event you attended in person was being broadcast live, and everyone around you was sharing photos on Snapchat, Instagram, or otherwise tweeting, posting, and communicating about the game through social networking sites. Advertising, marketing, branding, and sponsorship surrounded you throughout the event, some obvious, some not, but each bound by rules and regulations unbeknownst to most in the crowd. Even the stadium in which you sat is both economically and politically tied to that event you attended as a sport consumer.

Sport is big business. In fact, according to Statista, global sport revenue reached $500 billion in 2019. Sources of revenue for sport organizations include all the aspects mentioned above, and those most profitable

DOI: 10.4324/9781003031161-3

include television-broadcasting rights, and commercial sponsorships and endorsements—all of which are tied to advertisers, merchandise, spectator fees at events, and even tourism. This chapter reviews all of these revenue-generating facets because each is intricately tied to strategically communicating about and throughout the sport industry. Just as the example above conveys, every facet of sport or a sporting event experience is carefully planned out; every monetary exchange a purposeful partnership. This is because sports are valuable.

Tickets

One obvious revenue source for sporting events is ticket sales. Sport consumers purchase tickets to attend sporting events. The amount or percentage of a team's or a league's revenue that is generated by ticket sales varies widely. For example, the variance of ticket sales revenue across the major U.S. sports leagues range from 20 percent of total revenues in the National Basketball Association, to 60 percent in Major League Soccer.

Sport franchises offer ticket sales in a variety of formats. Ticket sales include single-game tickets, season tickets, group or other promotional game or series tickets, and some participate in secondary ticket sales. Season tickets are the most profitable form of ticket sales. Teams typically offer season ticket holders perks in games and hold promotional events for season ticket holders during the off-season or just before a new season kicks-off. Group rates, ticket giveaways, fire sales, coupon codes, and social media promotions are all common ways in which sport franchises promote ticket sales. Teams and stadiums also partner to offer package deals like suite sales. A stadium suite offers a large number of seats in a private room. Depending upon the agreement, suites even come equipped with a serving staff for meals and drinks. In the early 2000s, the Arizona Diamondbacks sold season suite packages to local businesses in the Phoenix area to bolster attendance at home games at the then-named Bank One Ballpark.

Table 2.1 Average per game attendance and ticket prices for five major U.S. leagues in 2019.

League	Attendance (avg per game)	Avg | Range Ticket Price	Total
NFL	66,151	range: $71–$166	avg: 4,696,721
NHL	17,456	$94	avg: 1,640,864
NBA	17,875	avg: $94 range: $58–$473	avg: 1,680,250
MLB	28,317	avg: $33	avg: 934,461
MLS	21,310	range: $16.47–$500	avg: 3,350,975.70

Sources: ESPN.com; Pfahler, 2017; Statista 2020; Yahoo! Finance, 2019.

Merchandise

Merchandise is another major source of revenue in global sport. Consumer behavior in sport, such as the purchase of sport merchandise, differs from most other industries. In sport, purchasing merchandise is all about wearing or displaying one's allegiance to sport (see "Fan Behaviors" in Chapter 3). Sport consumers thrive on wearing team logo apparel because it is an outward show of social identity, social support, and even a demonstration of boasting and celebration among fans. Sport merchandise also makes gift buying easy for the family member, friend, or workplace acquaintance who is a known sports fan.

Aside from gifting sport merchandise, research conducted on the National Hockey League revealed six factors that drive purchase intentions. Those six team-specific factors include: overall fan satisfaction, media exposure, on-field performance, the strength of a team's brand, the local market dynamics, and the purchaser's capacity to pay (O'Reilly et al., 2015). Sport merchandise can be purchased online, in stores, and at sporting events. But buyer beware: not all merchandise is created equal or are legal. Sport consumers should be careful to purchase official licensed merchandise.

Sponsorships and Endorsement

The partnerships and relationships that are established between a sport league, team, or athlete and a brand has value far beyond measureable dollars. The sponsoring brand pays to share reputational assets with the sport league, team, athlete, sporting event, or even a sport facility, stadium or arena. Sport sponsorships and endorsements are bidirectional in the reputational aspect. The brand awareness and recognition that can be acquired from such partnerships are of great worth and have long been deemed a reliable return on investment for the sponsoring brand as well as for the sport entity. Nevertheless, sponsorships and endorsements are the largest revenue category in sport.

In a general sense, sponsorships and endorsements can be distinguished by the sport entity. Sport sponsorships are typically larger scale: leagues, events, stadiums, or teams. Endorsements are more popular at the athlete level. This certainly does not indicate the amount of money exchanged is tiered in a similar way. Sport sponsorships power the sporting industry by providing billions of dollars. In fact, according to the IEG Sponsorship Report (2018), global sport sponsorships exceeded $62.7 billion in 2017, with a projected annual growth of 4–5 percent—which is a growth of approximately $2,821,500,000 each year. Sponsorships are intricately linked to marketing, and advertising as a component of marketing, both of which are discussed later in this chapter. Sport sponsorships allow companies to advertise their brand or logo at sporting events, on sport merchandise, or in virtually any other physical or digital form worked out within the sponsorship contract. It is important for strategic communicators to understand that contracts often forbid the display of other logos or contracts might offer other specific parameters around the use of logos. Knowing these rules and regulations are imperative to the success of any transmedia strategic communication campaign.

Endorsements are also high-dollar, reputation, or image exchanges. Endorsements are similar to sponsorships in that they connect brands with sport entities but endorsements allow brands to be showcased in a much more personalized way because the athlete endorses the brand as much as the brand endorses the athlete. "An endorsement grants the right to use (i.e., license) the athlete's name, image, or likeness in connection with advertising the sponsor's products or services" (US Legal, n.d.). Some leagues or sports have rules regarding endorsements. In the U.S., leagues prohibit endorsements from alcohol or tobacco companies, and the National Football League prohibits the endorsement of some nutritional supplements.

Endorsements often total more than salary for even the highest paid athletic stars. Out of all athletes around the world, tennis star Roger Federer enjoyed the highest endorsement income of $100 million in 2019 (Statista 2019/2020). Basketball star LeBron James and golfer Tiger Woods both tied for the second highest endorsement income of $60 million, each. Federer's profitable endorsements have been partnerships with several major brands: Nike, Wilson, Mercedes-Benz, Gillette, Barilla, Moët & Chandon, and Rimowa.

Brands choose sport sponsorships and endorsements to increase brand image, impact, recognition, credibility, and, of course, the bottom line (Woods, 2017). In fact, in 2018, 70 percent of the sponsorship market in North America was spent on sports. Nike is one of the most active brands in sponsorships and endorsements, and the brand's commitment to such partnerships have paid off well over the years. For example, Nike had a five-year, $1 billion sponsorship deal with the NFL to provide game day uniforms, which of course feature the recognizable Nike swoosh. Nike also endorsed Tiger Woods for a ten-year period, during which the company enjoyed increased golf ball sales. Ask yourself, when you think of your favorite sport or sporting event, what brand(s) come to mind?

Broadcasting Rights

Another major revenue source in sport are the broadcasting rights that media outlets purchase from sport leagues and franchises. Sports and media represents a hand-in-hand match with one another and media organizations have banked on this cohesion since radio was the only way the public could experience sport in real time other than physically attending a game. Over the years, television has become paramount. In fact, in 2017 there was 134,000 hours of sport broadcast airtime on television (Nielsen, 2018). Today, technological advances such as streaming and second screen use are now introducing new and exciting ways in which people consume sports and broadcasting rights are sold.

Broadcasting rights are sold to media entities in order for that partnered entity to broadcast the sport franchise's games, matches or competitions to a broader viewership than those in attendance. Broadcasting rights are beneficial to the media organization because of the increased viewers or listeners the sporting event draws in, and because of the ability to sell advertising around the sporting events being aired. For example, in 2020, Fox Sports sold 90 percent of its available advertising space for Major League Baseball games before the first game was played for the season (Ourand, 2020). Broadcasting collegiate football also is profitable when it comes to advertising. In fact, the NCAA's broadcasting partnership earns ESPN $792.5 million in annual advertising revenue (Crupisportico.com).

Broadcasting rights deals are intended to be another win–win revenue avenue but fees have skyrocketed over the years, narrowing profit margins for some media organizations. Broadcasting fees vary widely from league to league, too. For example, in 2017 the NFL collected $4 billion in broadcasting rights deals, while the NHL collected $220 million the same year (Magna; Axios). Over the years, leagues have found benefit in partnering with multiple media organizations. The WNBA has its longest-standing broadcasting partnership with ESPN. In more recent years, ABC joined in the broadcasting rights, and in 2020 the CBS Television Network was set to air its first ever WNBA broadcast—but just one game the whole season (Moran, 2019). The rest of the CBS deal would be broadcast on CBS's Sports Network.

In 2015, the NFL "broke new digital ground" when the league partnered with Yahoo! to livestream an NFL game played in London (NFL Communications, 2016). The following season featured a new "tri-cast" broadcast partnership that included Twitter in a league effort to celebrate fan use of second screens. After one season, Thursday Night Football was then broadcast via digital streaming on Amazon. This was a smart move given that 63 percent of sport consumers aged 18–24 watch sports on smartphones, laptops, or tablets (Activate; App Annie; Bloomberg; CBS; comScore, 2019), and this number across age groups only continues to grow. According to a 2020 report by *Sports Business Journal*, the NFL negotiated broadcasting rights with at least six different media organizations totaling $5 billion. These deals divvy up NFL game products. For example, ESPN purchased "Monday Night Football," Fox purchased Sunday afternoon games, DirecTV pays for the rights to "NFL Sunday Ticket," and NBC, ABC, and Verizon pay for rights for various other NFL broadcasts.

Another growing sport broadcasting phenomenon is that of league-specific media organizations. The NBA, MLB, NFL, and NHL all launched their own networks where their sport is featured around the clock. These networks partner with other sport-specific leagues and even purchase broadcasting rights to air events. NBA TV airs WNBA games, for example, and fans can purchase a WNBA League Pass for full access viewing (WNBA. com). In 2019, when the Alliance of American Football (AAF) launched, the league partnered with the NFL Network to broadcast several of its games in its inaugural season.

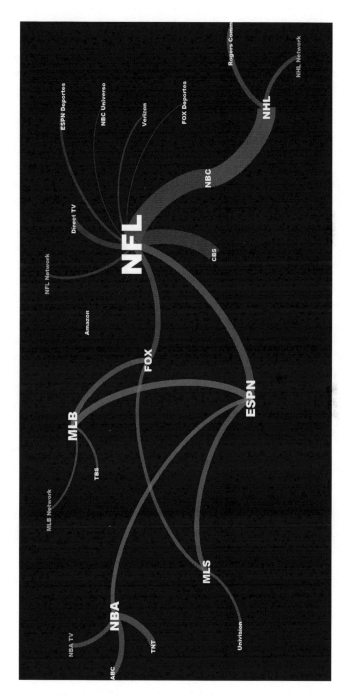

Figure 2.1 This sociogram demonstrates the 2017 U.S. major league sport and their respective broadcast rights deals with major media organizations.

Social Media as an Asset

Sports are additionally consumed through second screen use. Second screen devices such as smartphones, tablets, and personal computers are used to access additional content or to communicate with other fans regarding the televised or streaming sporting event being simultaneously consumed (Jensen et al., 2015). So, while a consumer is watching the game being broadcast on television or through a streaming service, those fans are also likely to be participating in second screen use. Social media is one major application of second screen use.

Social media has allowed for a wider, more diverse rhetorical arena within which to share thoughts, opinions, ideas, experiences, and unfortunately even misinformation and disinformation, regarding sports. Social media has also allowed fans to more intimately communicate with and interact with athletes, teams, leagues, and with each other. Sport fans share on social media when attending live events, too. As a mass communication channel, social media offers sport enterprises countless business opportunities for audience building and revenue generation.

Audience Building on Social Media

In 2019, the Alliance of American Football (AAF), a professional spring football league, launched in the U.S. Unfortunately, the league crumbled before the playoffs could begin during the inaugural season but the one thing the league did do well was utilize social media to build its brand. This now-defunct sports league taught American fans in the short time the league existed how to communicate about the AAF's league, teams, and game matchups in a more precise and consistent manner than any other U.S.-based sports league to date (Harker, 2021). The league was so successful with social media because the league was thoughtful in its creation of hashtags and then consistent in its use of hashtags. Hashtags are an anchoring rhetorical tool that conjoins topical conversations on social media and forms a "sports digital network" (Yan et al., 2018, p. 14). In other words, hashtags allow fans to connect to a larger conversation as it occurs worldwide and unfolds in real time.

The AAF provided fans and anyone else who wanted to discuss the league, its teams, and the weekly team matchups the specific hashtags to use in their conversations. The hashtags used purposeful key terms that promoted the league and its entities and activities. For example, the AAF's (league) hashtag was #JoinTheAlliance. This hashtag conveyed the call to action the league needed to communicate in its inaugural season: *join* us in this new football adventure of the *Alliance* of American Football. Each of the eight teams in the league all had its own hashtag, too, and those hashtags all remained the same from league inception throughout the end of the season. Team hashtags were created to mimic city, mascot, or tagline of the team. Then, each week, team matchups boasted hashtags linking the teams with city or state acronyms of each team linked with "vs" in the middle (e.g. #ORLvsSA).

Hashtags are social media currency and strategic communicators should seek legal protection for their league or team hashtags (i.e. trademark). One reason to seek legal protections is the phenomenon called "ambush marketing" (McKelvey & Grady, 2008). Ambush marketing is defined as "a practice whereby companies seek to associate or align themselves, in the mind of the public, with high-profile sports events and properties without paying the fees required to obtain official sponsor status" (p. 98). As you read above, sport sponsorship is a multi-billion dollar commitment. So, you can imagine the issues that might arise if some entity that has not invested financially for the right of use takes on the public benefits of sponsorship. For these reasons, every transmedia strategic communication campaign should include a section regarding the thoughtful consideration and a set of recommendations about legal protections.

Revenue Generation

Beyond the obvious promotions and sales pitches, social media allows leagues, teams, and athletes to intimately engage with fans and sponsors. For individual athletes, social media is another revenue generator outside of salary but connected to endorsements. Above, we discussed sponsorships and endorsements. Social media offers a platform for these revenue-generating sources to come together with sport to not only reach specific demographics and target audiences but also to interact and engage with them.

NUMBER OF FOLLOWERS

The number of social media account followers has fast become a measurement of success and potential across professions. The higher the number of followers, the greater the saturation is likely to be for a message on the social media platform, and therefore the more valuable. Cristiano Ronaldo, a professional soccer player for the Portugal national team, is the highest earning athlete on Instagram. Ronaldo boasted 224 million followers in summer 2020 and had 2,828 posts, though just one paid post earns him an estimated $975,000, according to a *Forbes* report (McCarthy, 2019). That article goes on to note that Ronaldo makes $47.8 million a year just from his Instagram activities. A recent photo of Ronaldo holding a Nike soccer cleat garnered 3.4 million hearts and 25,500 comments. That is an extensive reach for Nike's endorsement of Ronaldo and for just one social media post.

ENGAGEMENT OF FOLLOWERS

The interactivity of Ronaldo's Nike post is the perfect example of how imprecise social media metrics remain among strategic communicators. This is because strategic communicators use the term "engagement" to mean a million different things. When it comes to social media, no researcher or data analyst has yet nailed down the specific measurable aspects of social media engagement metrics. Instead, it may be best to approach social media from the perspective of interactivity in addition to engagement, each with varying weight.

The Ronaldo Nike soccer cleat post on Instagram that received 3.4 million hearts and 25,500 comments offers a great example regarding the difference between interactivity and engagement. The photo of Ronaldo and his Nike cleat received 3.4 million hearts. This is *interactivity* because 3.4 million people saw and interacted with his photo by clicking the heart button in response to his photo. What Nike is banking on, however, is *engagement* with Ronaldo's post from his 224 million followers. The caption with this particular photo reads: "Bringing back the Safari style from my first ever CR7 boots – 10 years later! What do you guys think? Collection now available on nike.com. #Mercurial #Safari." He asks, "What do you think?" and his followers left 25,500 comments sharing what they think.

Nike now knows through this engaging conversation how this shoe deal is being received amongst Ronaldo's followers because of the positive or negative sentiment within the comments his followers have left under the photo. To truly gauge how successful or unsuccessful this social media shoe deal with Ronaldo will be, Nike could have offered a unique link to and landing page for the new shoe on the Nike website for followers to purchase the shoes. Instead, Ronaldo simply wrote, "Collection now available on nike.com." Nike can still watch how many consumers visit the website to search for and purchase the shoe. Additionally, the website at the time required interested consumers to "Sign In to Buy" once they located the shoe which was featured in the "Just In" section. The followers who visit the Nike store and purchase the shoe are demonstrating true engagement, which is far more profitable than just banking on the heart interactivity on the Gram.

SOCIAL INFLUENCE

Social influence is a large part of what occurs on social media. Sport personas are no exception to this phenomenon. In fact, sport personas are among the highest paid social influencers and are among those with the largest number of followers. Social influencers are individuals who discuss a particular topic on social media and are viewed by followers as an expert on that topic. The expert thus socially influences others on matters pertaining to that topic. In sports, the leagues, teams, and athletes are perceived as experts on sport and neighboring topics related to sport. Due to the volume of followers that sport-related entities boast, sport-related social media accounts are easily transformed into influencer spouts. For example, during the COVID-19 pandemic in 2020, the National Football League and the National Football League Players Association could not come to an agreement regarding necessary health, safety, and financial amendments for the 2020 collective bargaining agreement. Reaching the end of their rope, players took to social media with the hashtag #WeWantToPlay. The hashtag quickly ignited, forcing the NFL to react to the moral outrage triggered by this act of social media influence and activism. By the next day, the two NFL entities announced they were closer to agreeing on how best to approach the 2020 season with protections in place for player health and safety during the COVID-19 pandemic.

Social media has allowed the public to participate in sports in a more intimate way than other forms of media allowed for in the past. This is because social media allows for conversations and two-way communication instead of the static one-way dissemination of broadcasting sports, alone. Sport franchises, as well as their corporate partners, are just scratching the surface on how to monetize these media platforms as revenue generators.

Sport Management

Sport management is a complex and intricate business. Sport management, also often referred to as sport administration, involves managing every business, finance, and personnel aspect of a particular sport franchise. Sport management degree programs teach aspiring front office staff about sport administration, legal considerations, marketing, facility and event management, compliance matters, and numerous other communication, broadcasting, and other technical operations. Sport management specifics varies depending upon the type of franchise or level of sport one manages. In the major leagues, for example, a commissioner is generally the top person who manages all the teams in a league as well as the league's operations and communication. Each team within a league are owned by individuals. Owners hire team managers to help run the daily business, finance, and personnel aspects of the team. Unfortunately, diversity in sport management is seriously lacking. American sports leagues are owned and managed by predominately wealthy white males. Sport also is made up of numerous governing bodies, so there are additional layers of compliance and management personnel overseeing the collegiate, professional or Olympic sport enterprises.

Strategic sport communication professionals must understand the complexities of managing a sport organization because sport organizations are multi-tiered, highly visible business operations.

The organizational flow of sport typically can be described from the macro to micro levels. At the macro level, there are global sports as a category or Olympics at the country level. At the meso level is sports leagues and sports teams. At the micro level are the individuals who participate within the sport industry, including coaches, coordinators, managers, trainers, and athletes, to name a few. Sport also features hierarchical levels from collegiate to professional. For example, there is collegiate sport, semi-professional or minor league sport, professional sport, and Olympic sport. Baseball encompasses a hierarchical progression, for example, from college baseball, to minor league baseball (MiLB), and then to Major League Baseball (MLB). In other words, American baseball players or coaches might begin in collegiate baseball as a preparatory experience for MiLB, and MiLB as preparatory league experience for the MLB. This progression is as much for athletes as for managers.

Knowing and accounting for the many layers and levels of sport are critical components to the creation and consideration of any strategic communication campaign.

Sport Economics

Sport economics is a broad concept that envelops the local-to-global economic impact of sport. Sport economics can include city–stadium agreements and taxpayer funding, the impact of sport on local businesses and area employment, travel and tourism, and sports betting. At the collegiate level, athletic departments operate on multi-million budgets and many such departments at major colleges and universities are economically self-sufficient due to the economic returns linked to some collegiate sports (i.e., football, basketball).

Sport Marketing

Marketing is defined as knowing your audience, knowing what they need and want, and then providing that audience with those needs and wants. Marketing is also defined as any promotional effort through which an organization provides valuable content, consistently, to a known target audience. In sport, marketing consistent content is literally the playing of the sport itself. So, every game in every season is a sport franchise's marketable content.

In 2019, the most valuable sporting events worldwide were the NFL Super Bowl ($780 million), the summer Olympics ($375 million), and the NCAA Men's Final Four basketball series ($300 million). Also in the top ten were the FIFA World Cup, WWE's WrestleMania, the Kentucky Derby, and, in tenth place, MLB's World Series (valued at $122 million). Each of these sporting events pairs with millions of viewers, and with billions in sponsorship opportunities. So, it is no wonder that sport marketing is among the most profitable in the world. Marketing in the major strategic sport communication umbrella that everything else falls under, including sponsorships and endorsements, advertising and public relations, and even social media and broadcasting rights. This is because every aspect of sport is marketable.

Advertising in Sport

Advertising falls under the sport marketing umbrella. Advertising is all about building awareness by paying for attention. Advertising is paid space, which is uniquely positioned in the sport industry. Consumers do not typically view sport promotions as advertising but sport franchises market and advertise events and merchandise just like any other business or organization.

Instead, sport consumers typically categorize advertising in sport as sport being the vessel through which advertisers reach consumers. This is one reason why sport is unique. Another reason is that sport is great at advertising itself without having to be pay but instead be paid. A classic example of how sport marketing, and thus advertising, turns dollars into sense in this way is best explained by the NFL's Super Bowl commercials phenomenon. The Super Bowl advertising revenue reached $336 million in 2019. The average cost of a 2019 Super Bowl 30-second advertisement was $5.25 million, and the highest paid advertising spend was $52 million by the NFL's biggest sponsor, Anheuser-Busch InBev (think, BudBowl). Not only is the NFL often allowed to weigh in on whether commercials will run or be cut, the league also negotiates the next year's broadcasting rights based off of the Super Bowl advertising revenue.

Sport Brands

Sport brands are incredibly profitable and marketable. The Real Madrid soccer team had the highest valued brand in sports in 2019, valued at $1.85 million (Statista, 2020). Branding alongside sport also falls under the marketing umbrella. Years of sponsorships and endorsements build brands over time. The sports-connected business brands that were ranked most valuable worldwide in 2019 include: Nike valued at $36.8 million, ESPN, Adidas, Gatorade, Sky Sports, Puma, Under Armour, UFC, YES, and Reebok valued at $.8 million (McCarthy, 2019; Statista, 2019).

Sport Law

Sport is rife with high-dollar contracts, celebrity status, and collective bargaining agreements. As such, the need for sport-specific laws has expanded over the years. Established laws regarding sport are numerous and complicated, so this section regarding sport law will remain focused on celebrity or public figure status, the right of publicity, and defamation. These topics represent the major areas of concern with which all strategic communicators should be familiar. This is because athletes and other sport personas are considered celebrity, and as such are recognized by the law as limited-purpose public figures or public figures. These categorizations provide few legal protections, and some came only after decades-long battles.

The *Right of Publicity* "makes it unlawful to use someone else's identity for commercial advantage without permission" (Sullivan, 2015). Recall once again here the discussions earlier in this chapter regarding sponsorships and endorsements. To use the image or likeness of a sport-related entity without permission is illegal and it devalues the negotiated contracts between sport entities, sponsors, and endorsers who paid large fees for the right of publicity. Right of publicity has been perhaps the biggest sport law story since the 1990s when a collegiate basketball player, Ed O'Bannon, sued the NCAA, and later the EA sports video game production company, for use of his image without compensation.

Defamation of character can happen to any person, including both public and private individuals. A person's character and reputation are valuable personal and professional assets. This is true for individuals who work in sport (Benoit, 2015; Kruse, 1981). Defamation cases concerning sport-related personnel are regularly brought to U.S. state and federal courts, and these cases are filed by professional and collegiate athletes as well as other sport personas.

Defamation is a spoken or written statement that an individual or entity knows is false but shares in some malicious manner anyway, and as a result injures the reputation or character of an individual (Veeder, 1903). Defamation is categorized as either libel or slander. Libel is a written form of defamation of character or a printed photograph or other printed representation such as a caricature. Slander is the spoken defamation of character. Defamation law is intended to protect the reputational assets of public officials, public figures, limited purpose public figures, and private citizens. Defamation claims are a legal recourse for purported harm to one's reputation. Recourse is carried out to recover a positive reputation, or in some cases financial loss, because an individual's reputation is considered a valuable, albeit "intangible" asset (Coombs, 2007, p. 164). It is required when a defamation suit is filed that the plaintiff establishes that the alleged defamation of character was an act of actual malice. Four main criteria must be met for a claim to be legally classified as defamation: 1) the statement must be undeniably proven false, 2) has been read or heard by a third party, 3) is harmful, and 4) must not fall under protected speech (Cotten & Wolohan, 2013).

Sport personas file defamation lawsuits not because they will win the lawsuit—they seldom win due to their classification as a public figure—but for the media coverage the filing of the lawsuit will create. This mediated coverage of the filed defamation claim allows a limited purpose public figure or a public figure to narrate the public discourse. To explain, the legal team files the defamation claim with the court and then the legal team sends out a media release to announce the suit was filed and why legal recourse is being sought. This strategy relies on press coverage to "set the record straight."

Sport law and media law often intertwine, and the right of publicity and defamation are only two examples of such. It is imperative that strategic communicators and sport managers know the law and integrate law-specific considerations into every strategic sport communication campaign.

Recommended additional readings

> Michael McCann, a sport law attorney, educator, and writer regularly published in *Sports Illustrated*. His articles can be accessed at this link: https://www.si.com/author/michael-mccann.
>
> Fields, S. K. (2016). *Game Faces: Sport Celebrity and the Laws of Reputation*. Champaign, IL: University of Illinois Press.
>
> Mitten, M. J., Davis, T., Osborne, B., & Duru, N. J. (2020). *Sports Law: Governance and Regulation*. Frederick, MD: Wolters Kluwer Law & Business.

Title IX

Title IX is another import law regarding sport. Title IX was passed in 1972 to address sex discrimination in sport. The law, which is 37 words in length, reads: "No person in the United States shall, on the basis of sex, be excluded from participation in, be denied the benefits of, or be subjected to discrimination under any education program or activity receiving Federal financial assistance."

Title IX addresses three specific areas regarding sex discrimination protections:

1. *Participation*: All individuals are to be allowed to participate in any sport.
2. *Treatment and benefits*: Fair, non-discriminatory treatment are to be offered to all who participate. There should be equal benefits for girls and women as are offered boys and men, regarding quality and access of uniforms, transportation, and field quality.
3. *Scholarships*: Equal access to and awarding of equitable athletic financial aid.

While Title IX has helped women and girls make great strides towards equality in sport, there is still much work to do. Experts note that Title IX, and the inequities the law attempts to address, still has a long way to go in achieving equitable solutions, and this is especially true for minority groups. The first step to improving the reach of Title IX is to learn about the law and to respect the law. Unfortunately, after nearly 50 years, more than half of Americans asked if they have heard of or know about Title IX report knowing not much or nothing at all (*Economist*, 2019, July 9).

Conclusion

This chapter has provided an overview of the business side of sport to show the many facets of sport management to consider when constructing a strategic sport communication campaign. From revenue sources and corporate partners to social media and sport marketing, the complexity of sport is an intriguing field of endless, profitable opportunity.

References

Anderson, J. (2019, November 12). Average ticket prices for each NBA team. Yahoo! Finance. Accessed online at https://finance.yahoo.com/news/average-ticket-prices-nba-team-100000563.html.

Badenhausen, K. (2020, July 31). The world's most valuable sports teams 2020. *Forbes*. Retrieved online at https://www.forbes.com/sites/kurtbadenhausen/2020/07/31/the-worlds-most-valuable-sports-teams-2020/?sh=56fa8a8c3c74.

Benoit, W. L. (2015). *Accounts, excuses, and apologies: Image repair theory and research* (2nd Ed.). Albany, NY: State University of New York Press.

Coombs, W. T. (2007). Protecting organization reputations during a crisis: The development and application of Situational Crisis Communication Theory. *Corporate Reputation Review, 10*(3), 163–176. http://doi.org/10.1057/palgrave.crr.1550049.

Cotten, D. J. & Wolohan, J. T. (2013). *Law for Recreation and Sport Managers* (6th Ed.). Dubuque, IA: Kendall/Hunt Publishing Co.

Economist, The (2019, July 5–9). *The Economist*/YouGov Poll, p. 185. Retrieved online at https://docs.cdn.yougov.com/al25duedar/econTabReport.pdf.

Harker, J. L. (2021). #JoinTheAlliance: A network exploration into hashtag brand-building by an emerging sports league. *Journal of Sports Media, 16*(1).

Jensen, J. A., Walsh, P., Cobbs, J., & Turner, B. A. (2015). The effects of second screen use on sponsor brand awareness: A dual coding theory perspective. *Journal of Consumer Marketing 32*(2), 71–84. https://doi.org/10.1108/JCM-02-2014-0861

Kruse, N. (1981). Apologia in team sport. *Quarterly Journal of Speech, 67*(3), 270–283. http://dx.doi.org/10.1080/00335638109383572.

McCarthy, N. (2019, October 28). The highest earners on Instagram. *Forbes.* Retrieved online at https://www.forbes.com/sites/niallmccarthy/2019/10/28/the-highest-earners-on-instagram-infographic/?sh=1d4199001110.

McKelvey, S., & Grady, J. (2008). Sponsorship program protection strategies for special sport events: Are event organizers outmaneuvering ambush marketers? *Journal of Sport Management, 22*(5), 550–586. https://doi.org/10.1123/jsm.22.5.550

Moran, E. (2019, August 2). First half viewership spike has WNBA Optimistic about 2019 and beyond. Front Office Sports. Accessed online at https://frntofficesport.com/wnba-viewership-growth/

Nielsen (2018). 2017 Year in sports media. Retrieved from https://www.neilsen.com/us/en/insihgts/report/2018/2017-year-in-sports-media/

NFL Communications (2016, April 5). National Football League and Twitter announce streaming partnership for Thursday night football. NFL. Retrieved online at https://nflcommunications.com/Pages/National-Football-League-and-Twitter-Announce-Streaming-Partnership-for-Thursday-Night-Football.aspx

O'Reilly, N., Foster, G., Murray, R., & Shimizu, C. (2015). Merchandise sales rank in professional sport: Purchase drivers and implications for National Hockey League clubs. *Sport, Business and Management, 5*(4), 307–324. https://doi.org/10.1108/SBM-10-2012-0044

Ourand, J. (2020, July 22). Fox sells 90% of ad inventory for shortened MLB season. *Sports Business Daily.* Accessed online at https://www.sportsbusinessdaily.com/Daily/Morning-Buzz/2020/07/22/MLB-ad-sales-Fox.aspx.

Pfahler, L. (2017, November 28). Taking a look at what Major League Soccer teams charge for tickets. WPCO.com. Accessed online at https://www.wcpo.com/news/insider/taking-a-look-at-what-major-league-soccer-teams-charge-for-tickets.

Statista (2019, October 19). Most valuable sports business brands worldwide in 2019. Retrieved online at https://www.statista.com/statistics/253349/brand-value-of-sports-businesses-worldwide/.

Sullivan, R. (2015). An athlete's right of publicity: An active area in sports law. Accessed online at https://heitnerlegal.com/2015/06/12/an-athletes-right-of-publicity-an-active-area-in-sport-law/

US Legal. (n.d.) Sports law. Sports contracts – basic principles. Accessed online at https://sportslaw.uslegal.com/sports-agents-and-contracts/sports-contracts-basic-principles/

Veeder, V. V. (1903). The history and theory of the law of defamation. *Columbia Law Review, 3*(8), 546–573. http://www.jstor.org/stable/1109121

WNBA.com. https://www.wnba.com/national-tv-schedule/

Woods, L. (2017, Sept. 26). Why Nike uses endorsements & sponsorships. BizFluent. Accessed online at https://bizfluent.com/13636879/why-nike-uses-endorsements-sponsorships.

Yan, G., Watanabe, N. M., Shapiro, S. L., Naraine, M. L., & Hull, K. (2018). Unfolding the Twitter scene of the 2017 UEFA Champions League Final: Social media networks and power dynamics. *European Sport Management Quarterly*, 1–18. https://doi.org/10.1080/16184742.2018.1517272

3   Sports Fans

There are few genres of fans that are more fanatical than sports fans. This chapter discusses what makes a fan a fan, explores the psychological and behavioral tendencies of sports fans, and discusses how a deep understanding of sports fans should shape any strategic sport communication message you develop.

To explain the latter, the TNT approach demonstrates how we filter messages through our own array of past experiences, perceptions, and personal preferences. For a sports fan, a deep identification with a favorite sport or a favorite team can result in a deep personal, or even parasocial, connection through which all messaging is filtered. These filters shape and reshape the message sent by the communicator. For example, a sports fan will assign sentiment to strategic sport communication messages. This assigned sentiment will be either positive or negative depending upon that fan's perceptions and identification related to the topic at hand. Sentiment is a subjective feeling or expression and differs from one individual to the next. Sentiment varies in valence (positive or negative) and also varies in degree or severity. For example, a positive sentiment can be weak (that team is OK, I would watch them play a game) to strong (this is my favorite team, I never miss a game!). Sentiment will be assigned to the perception of the message being sent, and sentiment will be evidenced in any communicated action that follows (e.g., discordant communication).

This chapter explains the key aspects of being a sports fan so that strategic communicators can consider the many filters their messages must pass through and how those messages might be reassigned or co-created in meaning, and then expression.

Be[com]ing a Sports Fan

Becoming a sports fan occurs in multiple ways. Some people are raised in sport-centric families, for example, where attending or watching sporting events are a part of everyday family life. Some people become sports fans later in life. For example, women demonstrate the most overt fandom during their college years. There have been debates regarding whether being or becoming a fan of sport is a natural *trait* or propensity for some people, or

DOI: 10.4324/9781003031161-4

whether it is a *state* that one grows into through their social interactions. This may remain a question for the ages but in this chapter we will discuss what we know so far regarding the road to fandom.

Regardless of how one becomes a fan, interactions with sport can result in increased identification. This is what the whole purpose of this book is about. It will become your job to explore the why and how and who regarding sports and ultimately be able to identify how to increase interaction and thus support. Some might hypothesize that the more interpersonal the interactions with a sports team, the more "die-hard" the fan will become. For example, researchers have noted that the amount of time involved or the frequencies of interactions that occur are components that translate into identification (Larkin, Fink, & Trail, 2015; Mael & Ashforth, 1992). This is because personal experiences contribute to personal identification (Hirt & Clarkson, 2011), and interactions build trust, which is also important for continued involvement (Harpham, 2008). Personal involvement, and thus identification, is nurtured through socialization with parents, partners, siblings, friends, school, and community throughout an individual's life (Funk & James, 2001).

A sports fan is defined as a follower of sport who is actively interested and engaged with sport (Wann, 2006). The word "fan" comes from the word "fanatic" which puts an "emphasis on emotion over knowledge" (Hirt & Clarkson, 2011, p. 2). Sports fans report high levels of enjoyment from sport consumption, they consume sport media for an hour or more a day, and they actively seek out sport information (Gantz et al., 2006).

In this book, we break down being a sports fan into two wide categories: fanship and fandom. We operationalize *fanship* as a personal identification with a favorite team or sport. We operationalize *fandom* as a larger social identification of being a fan of sport, at-large.

Fanship

Fanship is described as a continuum (Wann & Branscombe, 1993; Gantz, Wang, Paul, & Potter, 2006), and "represents an array of thought processes, affective attachments, and behaviors that separate fans from nonfans" (Gantz, Wang, Paul, & Potter, 2006, p. 96). Fanship is demonstrated through personal involvement and engagement. This includes behaviors like: thinking about sports, talking with friends about sports, planning one's personal schedule around sports, socializing around sports—even planning to go to a restaurant or bar to watch sports, and finally, wearing branded or logo sport-related apparel such as t-shirts, hats, etc. (see BIRGing in the list of fan behaviors below).

Fandom

Fandom can best be described as a group identity. To explain, following is an overview of how social identity, social comparison, and superiority all mix together in sport fandom. You will be able to identify components of each when you read about fan behavior in the next section.

Social identification describes a portion of a person's self-concept within a larger group. Several characteristics of social identification are each sensibly applicable to sport: internalization of belonging, group comparisons focused on certain attributes, out-group comparisons with a worthy opponent, and superiority maintenance (Tajfel & Turner, 1979). Social identification is deeply rooted in social comparison, which strengthens as in-group distinctiveness grows. For example, being part of a socially favorable group offers superiority over other less successful out-groups (Ashforth & Mael, 1989; Wann, 2006; Wann & Branscombe, 1995). Losing rival teams offer sports fans of the winning team this in-group distinctiveness of being part of the socially favorable group, making identification and involvement more enjoyable. This is because superiority is an important characteristic in maintaining a positive social identification. A fan relationally compares one's own team record to the rival team's record and resultantly feels more or less personally successful as a result of such comparison (Tajfel & Turner, 1979). This comparative, socially relational identification to others connected to the same winning team—or distinctiveness from the losing rival team—is what defines sport fandom.

Webster's Dictionary defines fandom as "being a fan (of a particular person, place, thing) regarded collectively as a community or subculture." Fandom is therefore a social identification with other fans with a nod toward a collective esteem (Dietz-Uhler & Murrell, 1999; Reysen & Branscombe, 2010). In other words, fandom is a social identification that is at its root an attempt to attach oneself to a positively perceived group. Fandom therefore meets three central underlying needs: validation, pleasure, and arousal (Hirt & Clarkson, 2011). These three needs vary greatly among individuals, with gender being one of the most prominent differing factors.

Gender Differences among Sports Fans

For example, companionship and the sociability of watching sports and attending games differ vastly between males and females. Males score higher in fanship level (individual identification) and women in fandom levels (group identification) due to the sociability of fandom (Dietz-Uhler, Harrick, End, & Jacquemotte, 2000; Gantz & Wenner, 1991, 1995; Wenner & Gantz, 1998). Dietz-Uhler et al. (2000) noted that men and women are equally sports fans, but men identify and engage more with sport than women. Women prefer to engage in sport with friends and family (Dietz-Uhler et al., 2000; Wann, Schrader, & Wilsen, 1999; Wenner & Gantz, 1998), whereas men engage for the entertainment of sport and for economic motivation (Wann, Schrader, & Wilsen, 1999).

Building Fan Identification

Building identification among all sports fans is *your* job. The overall transmedia strategic sport communication campaign you create should take all of these facets into consideration. Any interpersonal interaction, such as community events or social media exchanges, because interpersonal exchanges hold the highest currency in increasing identification and building fan support. Still, though, sports fan act out in overt ways and it is imperative to understand that some have a higher propensity to do so than others. The state vs. trait conversation runs deep here.

Some might argue that sport identification is a distinct function from the personality traits that may predict certain types of fan behavior (Brown-Devlin, Devlin, & Vaughan, 2018). Whether one in the same or distinctly different, the research still suggests that knowing the personality propensities of sports fans can help marketers better strategize ticket sales and fan experiences. Personality traits as predictors of fanship or fandom additionally leads to declared propensities for certain fan behavior (Brown-Devlin & Devlin, 2020). For example, those who score high on sociability and sincerity in personality tests may be more likely to demonstrate publicly their fanship for their favorite team (Brown-Devlin & Devlin, 2020), while others have also noted a social conscientiousness as antecedent to rivalry discordant communication (Harker & Jensen, 2020).

The next section explains the numerous fan behaviors that scholars have named and researched over the years, while parsing out such psychological antecedents from the behavioral outcomes of these fan behaviors. Fan behavior is an important consideration when developing campaign messages and deciding upon target audiences for those messages.

Fan Behavior

Fans act out in overt ways. From painted naked bodies in freezing temperatures to the superstitions of wearing a favorite hat, sports fans can perhaps be just as fun a sideshow as the sport itself. Of course, not all sports fan behavior is good and sometimes sports fans' behaviors can get downright dangerous. Hooliganism, for example, is a fan behavior coined in international soccer that describes the mob mentality and destruction that occurs in and around sports arenas. Hooliganism has been perhaps best explained in Frosdick and Marsh's (2013) book titled *Football Hooliganism*, where the authors discuss the violence and vandalism historically connected to such behaviors by football fans.

Here, we define a number of fan behaviors that have been named and discussed over the past four or five decades by U.S. scholars. Each of these behaviors displayed by sports fans are rooted in psychological and sociological underpinnings. This means that sports makes people feel feelings and then those feelings are expressed in several distinct ways. These overt behaviors includes communication—how sports fans speak to each other, for example—but as you will read in the following list, fan behavior also includes what people choose to wear, how they act, and even how they might avoid reading or watching the news.

Researchers have observed and named many forms of fan behavior. Interestingly, fan behavior research took on a unique form is naming fan behavior by using acronyms to describe the behavior. Below is a list of fan behavior acronyms, what they stand for, and how research came to recognize and research each.

BIRGing

BIRGing (basking in reflective glory) is an outward display of an individual's fanship for their favorite team by wearing team logo apparel or displaying team logo memorabilia in their home or office.

More specifically, researchers define BIRGing as a demonstrated image management strategy by wearing a team's logo apparel following a winning game. Researchers at several American universities observed students wearing school-related logo apparel when attending classes on the Mondays following winning Saturday football games. The researchers hypothesized that a collegiate football team's victory causes university students to identify more positively and overtly with their institution by wearing "school-identifying apparel" (Cialdini et al., 1976, p. 370). BIRGing is a physical display of vicarious achievement (Campbell et al., 2004) but the positive social identity gained from BIRGing also couples with communication cues such as the use of the words "we" and "us" when talking about or reminiscing about a team win (Cialdini et al., 1976; Jensen et al., 2016). Even in death, BIRGing continues among sports fans, as one study has demonstrated (Campbell et al., 2021).

CORFing

CORFing (cutting off reflected failure) is an attempt to bury the shame and regret of being connected to a losing team by avoiding news and highlights the force the sports fan to relive the loss.

Fans of losing teams attempt to maintain a positive identity by "cutting off reflected failure" or CORFing (Wann & Branscombe, 1990). Fans who CORF demonstrate a regressive tendency toward media use and information-seeking (Dietz-Uhler & Murrell, 1999; Jensen et al., 2016; Spinda, 2011) due to the resultant blasting that is common when fans of a winning team teases rival losers (Spinda, 2011). This regressive media use, combined with the absence of BIRGing following a loss (Jensen et al., 2016), is due to a perceived "less favorable social identity" when openly connecting themselves to a losing team (End et al., 2002, p. 1019). Studies have documented that the higher a person's sport identification, the less likely the fan is to CORF (Billings et al., 2017; Wann & Branscombe, 1990). Conversely, lower levels of sport identification correlates with the higher likelihood of CORFing behaviors (Billings et al., 2017; Spinda, 2011; Wann & Branscombe, 1990). Wann and Branscombe (1990) suggested that those who CORF are those who may be responsible for game attendance fluctuations following winning or losing seasons; however, no longitudinal study has captured this specific data.

COFFing

Cutting off future failure is the pessimistic reluctance to admit one's fanship for a team enduring a long-term losing streak.

An extension of CORFing is COFFing, or cutting off future failure, which is a distancing, protective image management strategy that protects oneself from perceived future social identity damage by not overtly sharing with others an admiration for a losing team (Wann et al., 1995). Indeed, COFFing is a self-preservation attempt that connects group identification and personal self-esteem (End et al., 2002; Hirt, Zillman, Erickson, & Kennedy, 1992).

BIRFing and *CORSing*

On the flip side of COFFing, we have BIRFing and CORSing. In 2004, Campbell expanded the fan behavior literature by adding BIRFing (basking in reflected failure) and CORSing (cutting off reflected success). Both of these fan behaviors are akin to the "die-hard" or long-time/life-long fan. A perfect example are Chicago Cubs fans, who are situated within these behaviors for the unwavering support they continued to offer the team even after enduring over 100 years of not winning the World Series. The Cubs finally won in 2016 after a century-long dry spell since their 1907 and 1908 wins. Time is a measurement of BIRFing, and CORSing is mostly connected to a continued rooting for the "underdog."

COATing and *FASTing*

Jensen et al. (2016) offered a reasonable expansion to BIRGing and CORFing by suggesting a revised operationalization of each to COATing (celebrating our accomplishment together) and FASTing (failure to achieve a shared triumph). These two newest suggested fan behavior acronyms are a nod to the social sharing of successes and loses related to sport. The authors of this replication study, conducted 40 years after Cialdini's first BIRGing study, explain fans are experiencing collective feelings and not just reflective feelings. Jensen et al. (2016) goes on to convey that sport fans likely feel they contribute in meaningful ways through their dedication to following along: cheering from afar when unable to actually attend games and collectively gathering and communicating in person or online.

Fan Behaviors Exchanged between Rival Fans

One of the most fun facets of being a sports fan is the banter shared among like fans or between rival fans. Above, you read about fan behaviors that are rooted in the individual's feelings or quest for a positively perceived social image. Here, we discuss the negative feelings toward, and the direct communicated attacks shared between, rival fans of sport.

Blasting (Cialdini & Richardson, 1980)

We are learning that discordant communication could be a form of social support in sport communication. Blasting, or trash talking, other sports fans is a regular component of sport fandom and fanship. Blasting is defined as an out-group derogation and was the second image management strategy within the family of fan behaviors to be explained and developed regarding sports and sports fans (Cialdini & Richardson, 1980). Sports fans will bolster, or speak positively, of their own favorite team and will use explicit negative words regarding a rival team (Spinda, 2011). Wann and Dolan (1994) note that this banter between rival fans is rooted more in the strong positive connection with their favorite team's in-group, and not necessarily motivated by the fan's desire to derogate the out-group rival team's fans. Harker and Jensen (2020) argue that it is in fact the sports fan's perception of a rival fan's level of fanship, or sport identification, with a rival team that is a predictor of the blasting fan behavior. Regardless, a fan's team performing well triggers a fan's blasting, or a rival performing poorly triggers blasting and the fan boasts over that perceived superiority.

GORFing (Havard, 2014)

GORFing (glory out of reflected failure) is a form of gloating, yet much less overt. GORFing is an extension of blasting and is also exhibited between rival fans, but GORFing occurs during times of indirect competition. Four major themes surrounding GORFing emerged from Havard's work on this fan behavior: socialization, in-group bias, sense of satisfaction, and out-group indirect competition (Havard, 2014). GORFing was later empirically extended by examining four affective measurements that included happiness, satisfaction, relief, and pride (Billings et al., 2017). GORFing in the Billings study is a measurement of internal, individual feelings about a rival team losing to another rival team and in no way reflects actual communication between fans. Harker and Jensen (2020) examined self-reported communication exchanges between rival fans and found disidentification to play a major role in whether and with whom rival discussant would be chosen. The motivating factor for communication interaction was not the sports fan's own fanship but instead their perception of the rival fan's level of fanship. Both of these recent studies combine GORFing with the application of schadenfreude, which is a feeling of joy at another's adversity (Heider 1958), which is discussed next.

Schadenfreude

Schadenfreude has only in the past decade or so been assigned to sport fan behavior. As mentioned above, schadenfreude is defined as the feeling of joy at another's adversity (Cikara, 2011; Cikara & Fiske, 2012; Harker & Jensen, 2020; Heider, 1958; Leach et al. 2003, 2015; Leach & Spears, 2009).

Schadenfreude in response to sports is a reactive inferiority threat, typically displayed between rival sports fans (Harker & Jensen 2020; Leach et al., 2003).

Schadenfreude is imagined in three ways: when a misfortune befalls an envied person; the misfortune is perceived as deserved; and when something might be gained for the observer from that misfortune (Cikara & Fiske, 2012). Schadenfreude has been measured with several emotion measurements including joy, happiness, relief, satisfaction, pride, gloating, sympathy, sadness, and envy (Leach et al., 2015; Leach & Spears 2009; Leach et al., 2003). Perhaps the most intriguing investigation of schadenfreude and sport is the Cikara et al. (2011) MRI brain scans study of baseball fans' reactions as they watched plays and game outcomes of their favorite and rival baseball teams. Results demonstrated that sports fans activated the area of the brain for happiness when their favorite or favored team played well or won a game but also demonstrated slightly higher levels of happiness when a rival team lost or played poorly. Just as intriguing, the anger and pain areas of the brain lit up when a fan's favorite team lost or when a rival team won.

Schadenfreude has been found to stretch beyond the joy emotion and spill into the expression of pride and superiority by directly insulting rival fans by engaging in discordant communication (Harker & Jensen, 2020). This is why schadenfreude is hypothetically harmful to social relationships: because it creates an antagonistic relationship (Heider, 1958). But is it really all that bad to feel and express schadenfreude in relation to sport?

One might argue that sport consumption and sport consumerism are fan behaviors. They are certainly linked to BIRGing and CORFing, and are likely driven by fanship or fandom or both. It is important to understand the difference between sport consumption and sport consumerism.

Sport consumption is quite literally the consumption of sport. A person is consuming sports when s/he attends a sporting event, watches sports on TV, listens to sports on the radio, reads about sports in the newspaper, or reads tweets or posts about something related to sports on Twitter or some other social media platform. Sport consumerism is defined as any sports-related purchase, which can include sport consumption. Sport consumerism ranges from the purchase of sports trading cards and jerseys to subscriptions to sports league networks or game day tickets. Sport consumerism is big business around the world. In fact, in 2017 in the U.S. alone, more than $100 billion was spent consuming sports (Katz, 2017).

Conclusion

To recap, fan behaviors range from wearing a favorite team's logo to hurling insults at rival fans. Because of these overt behaviors, it usually isn't too diffi-cult to identify sports fans, whether they are "die-hard" or "fair-weathered" fans. Understanding how fans behave is helpful in understanding how to communicate with sports fans across platforms using the TNT approach. Understanding how fans behave is also helpful in constructing strategic com-munication campaigns focused on increasing sport consumption and sport consumerism. As you develop your plans, we ask you to consider: *Which fan behaviors have you participated in over the years? What fan behavior would you add to these lists? How will your campaign consider both sport consumption and sport consumerism in its TNT approach?*

References

Ashforth, B. E., & Mael, F. (1989). Social identity theory and the organization. *Academy of Management Review, 14*(1), 20–39. http://dx.doi.org/10.5465/AMR.1989.4278999

Billings, A. C., Qiao, F., Brown, K. A., & Devlin, M. (2017). Fandom, rival successes and failures, and the introduction of glory out of reflected failure measurements. In A. C. Billings & K. A. Brown. (Eds.). *Evolution of the modern sport fan: Communicative approaches* (pp. 65–82). London: Lexington Books.

Brown-Devlin, N., & Devlin, M. B. (2020). Winning with personality: Underscoring antecedents for college students' motives for team identification. *Communication & Sport, 8*(3), 364–388. https://doi.org/10.1177%2F2167479519832017

Brown-Devlin, N., Devlin, M. B., & Vaughan, P. W. (2018). Why fans act that way: Using individual personality to predict BIRGing and CORFing behaviors. *Communication & Sport.* https://doi.org/10.1177/2167479517725011

Campbell, J., Dandignac, M., Bankert, C., Hall, C., McArthur, K., Sessions, B., & Young, C. (2021). Die-hard fans: Selective self-presentation in newspaper obituaries. *Mortality, 26*(1), 112–123. https://doi.org/10.1080/13576275.2020.1784122

Campbell, R. M., Aiken, D., & Kent, A. (2004). Beyond BIRGing and CORFing: Continuing the exploration of fan behavior. *Sport Marketing Quarterly, 13*(3), 151–157.

Cialdini, R. B., & Richardson, K. D. (1980). Two indirect tactics of image management: Basking and blasting. *Journal of Personality and Social Psychology, 39*(3), 406–415. http://dx.doi.org/10.1037/0022-3514.39.3.406

Cialdini, R. B., Borden, R. J., Thorne, A., Walker, M. R., Freeman, S., & Sloan, L. R. (1976). Basking in reflected glory: Three (football) field studies. *Journal of Personality and Social Psychology, 34*(3), 366–375. http://dx.doi.org/10.1037/0022-3514.34.3.366

Cikara, M., & Fiske, S. T. (2012). Stereotypes and Schadenfreude: Affective and physiological markers of pleasure at outgroup misfortunes. *Social Psychological and Personality Science, 3*(1), 63–71. https://doi.org/10.1177/1948550611409245

Cikara, M., Botvinick, M. M., & Fiske, S. T. (2011). Us versus them: Social identity shapes neural responses to intergroup competition and harm. *Psychological Science, 22*(3), 306–313. https://doi.org/10.1177/0956797610397667

Dietz-Uhler, B., & Murrell, A. (1999). Examining fan reactions to game outcomes: A longitudinal study of social identity. *Journal of Sport Behavior, 22*(1), 15–27. Retrieved from http://libproxy.lib.unc.edu/login?url=https://search.proquest.com/docview/215876024?accountid=14244

Dietz-Uhler, B., Harrick, E., End, C., & Jacquemotte, L. (2000). Sex differences in sports fan behavior and reasons for being a sport fan. *Journal of Sport Behavior, 23*(3), 219–231. Retrieved from http://libproxy.lib.unc.edu/login?url=https://search.proquest.com/docview/1311960912?accountid=14244

End, C. M., Dietz-Uhler, B., Harrick, E. A., & Jacquemotte, L. (2002). Identifying with winners: A reexamination of sport fans' tendency to BIRG. *Journal of Applied*

Social Psychology, 32(5), 1017–1030. https://doi.org/10.1111/j.1559-1816.2002.tb00253.x

Frosdick, S., & Marsh, P. (2013). *Football hooliganism.* New York: Routledge.

Funk, D. C., & James, J. (2001). The psychological continuum model: A conceptual framework for understanding an individual's psychological connection to sport. *Sport Management Review, 4*(2), 119–150. https://doi.org/10.1016/S1441-3523(01)70072-1

Gantz, W., & Wenner, L. A. (1991). Men, women, and sport: Audience experiences and effects. *Journal of Broadcasting & Electronic Media, 35*(2), 233–243. https://doi.org/10.1080/08838159109364120

Gantz, W., & Wenner, L. A. (1995). Fanship and the television sport viewing experience. *Sociology of Sport Journal, 12*(1), 56–74. https://doi.org/10.1123/ssj.12.1.56

Gantz, W., Wang, Z., Paul, B., & Potter, R. F. (2006). Sport versus all comers: Comparing TV sport fans with fans of other programming genres. *Journal of Broadcasting & Electronic Media, 50*(1), 95–118. https://doi.org/10.1207/s15506878jobem5001_6

Harker, J. L., & Jensen, J. A. (2020). Adding insult to rivalry: Exploring the discord communicated between rivals. *International Journal of Sports Marketing and Sponsorship, 21*(4), 633–649. https://doi.org/10.1108/IJSMS-12-2019-0141

Harpham, T. (2008). The measurement of community social capital through surveys. In I. Kawachi, S. V. Subramanian, & D. Kim (Eds.) *Social Capital and Health* (pp. 51–62). New York: Springer.

Havard, C. T. (2014). Glory out of reflected failure: The examination of how rivalry affects sport fans. *Sport Management Review, 17*(3), 243–253. https://doi.org/10.1016/j.smr.2013.09.002

Heider, F. (1958). The naive analysis of action. In F. Heider, *The psychology of interpersonal relations* (pp. 79–124). John Wiley & Sons Inc. https://doi.org/10.1037/10628-004

Hirt, E. R., & Clarkson, J. J. (2011). The psychology of fandom: Understanding the etiology, motives, and implications of fanship. In L. R. Kahle & A. G. Close (Eds.) *Consumer behavior knowledge for effective sport and event marketing* (pp. 59–85). New York: Routledge.

Hirt, E. R., Zillmann, D., Erickson, G. A., & Kennedy, C. (1992). Costs and benefits of allegiance: Changes in fans' self-ascribed competencies after team victory versus defeat. *Journal of Personality and Social Psychology, 63*(5), 724–738. http://dx.doi.org/10.1037/0022-3514.63.5.724

Jensen, J. A., Turner, B. A., James, J., McEvoy, C., Seifried, C., Delia, E., …, & Walsh, P. (2016). Forty years of BIRGing: New perspectives on Cialdini's seminal studies. *Journal of Sport Management, 30*(2), 149–161. https://doi.org/10.1123/jsm.2015-0340

Katz, J. (Sept. 17, 2017). $100 billion—that's how much Americans spent on sports over the past 12 months. *MarketWatch.* Accessed online at https://www.marketwatch.com/story/heres-how-much-americans-spend-on-sports-in-one-chart-2017-09-11

Larkin, B., Fink, J. S., & Trail, G. T. (2015). An examination of constraints and motivators as predictors of sport media consumption substitution intention. *Sport Marketing Quarterly, 24*(3), 183–197. Retrieved from http://libproxy.lib.unc.edu/login?url=https://search.proquest.com/docview/1710602722?accountid=14244

Leach, C. W., & Spears, R. (2009). Dejection at in-group defeat and schadenfreude toward second-and third-party out-groups. *Emotion, 9*(5), 659–665. http://dx.doi.org/10.1037/a0016815

Leach, C. W., Spears, R., & Manstead, A. S. (2015). Parsing (malicious) pleasures: Schadenfreude and gloating at others' adversity. *Frontiers in Psychology, 6*, 201. https://doi.org/10.3389/fpsyg.2015.00201

Leach, C. W., Spears, R., Branscombe, N. R., & Doosje, B. (2003). Malicious pleasure: Schadenfreude at the suffering of another group. *Journal of Personality and Social Psychology, 84*(5), 932–943. http://dx.doi.org/10.1037/0022-3514.84.5.932

Mael, F., & Ashforth, B. E. (1992). Alumni and their alma mater: A partial test of the reformulated model of institutional identification. *Journal of Institutional Behavior, 13*(2), 103–123. https://doi.org/10.1002/job.4030130202

Reysen, S., & Branscombe, N. R. (2010). Fanship and fandom: Comparisons between sport and non-sport fans. *Journal of Sport Behavior, 33*(2), 176–193. Retrieved from http://libproxy.lib.unc.edu/login?url=https://search.proquest.com/docview/215872141?accountid=14244

Spinda, J. S. (2011). The development of basking in reflected glory (BIRGing) and cutting off reflected failure (CORFing) measures. *Journal of Sport Behavior, 34*(4), 392–420. Retrieved from http://libproxy.lib.unc.edu/login?url=https://search.proquest.com/docview/903983079?accountid=14244

Tajfel, H., & Turner, J. C. (1979). An integrative theory of inter-group conflict. In W. G. Austin & S. Worchel (Eds.), *The social psychology of inter-group relations* (pp. 33–47). Monterey, CA: Brooks/Cole.

Wann, D. L. (2006). Understanding the positive social psychological benefits of sport team identification: The team identification-social psychological health model. *Group Dynamics: Theory, Research, and Practice, 10*(4), 272–296. http://dx.doi.org/10.1037/1089-2699.10.4.272

Wann, D. L. (1995). Preliminary validation of the sports fan motivation scale. *Journal of Sport & Social Issues, 19*(4), 377–396. http://dx.doi.org/10.1177/019372395019004004

Wann, D. L., & Branscombe, N. R. (1993). Sport fans: Measuring degree of identification with their team. *International Journal of Sport Psychology, 24*, 1–17.

Wann, D. L., & Branscombe, N. R. (1990). Die-hard and fair-weather fans: Effects of identification on BIRGing and CORFing tendencies. *Journal of Sport and Social issues, 14*(2), 103–117. https://doi.org/10.1177/019372359001400203

Wann, D. L., & Dolan, T. J. (1994). Spectators' evaluations of rival and fellow fans. *The Psychological Record, 44*(3), 351–358.

Wann, D. L., Melnick, M. J., Russell, G. W., & Pease, D. G. (2001). *Sport fans: The psychology and social impact of spectators.* New York: Routledge.

Wann, D., Schrader, M., & Wilsen, A. (1999). Sports fan motivation: Questionnaire validation, comparisons by sport, and relationship to athletic motivation. *Journal of Sport Behavior, 22*(1), 114–139. Retrieved from http://libproxy.lib.unc.edu/login?url=https://search.proquest.com/docview/1311944262?accountid=14244

Wenner, L. A., & Gantz, W. (1998). Watching sport on television: Audience experience, gender, fanship, and marriage. In L. A. Wenner (Ed.). *MediaSport* (pp. 233–251). New York: Routledge.

4   Scanning and Monitoring

Models of the strategic communication process are rough maps that guide you through the process of creating messages for an organization. We use the term rough map because it is not a detailed checklist of what you have to do but rather list of points you need to consider. Seasoned professionals know the process and it comes to them automatically. Novice strategic communicators need some guidance to learn the process. Most models of strategic communication begin with research. However, that assumes you somehow know what you want to research. This is no problem if you are executing a specific communication effort that your organization does regularly such as posting to a social media platform. But how do you discover new ideas to add to your strategic communication efforts? The answer to that is scanning.

You have been doing scanning most of your life but just not called it that. When you learned to cross the street, you are taught to stop, look left, look right, and look left before crossing. In some countries you look right, look left, and look right. In London, for instance, look right is painted on the street to help tourists. Looking before crossing the street is scanning. Scanning is when you search the environment for information. In this chapter we present the basic points you need to know for scanning. We begin the chapter by defining scanning then moving to some techniques that can facilitate the process and conclude with deliverables created at the end of the scanning stage.

Scanning Defined

Scanning is also known as environmental scanning and helps managers to develop strategy—decide what to do in the future. Scanning is a systematic search of the environment for information that is relevant to the organization. The environment includes searching for information both inside and outside of the organization. Not only does scanning find information but it needs to interpret that information. Information is just data and has no real value until you interpret/analyze the information. Imagine you have conducted a focus group of season ticketholders to learn more about what motivates their purchasing. If you simply transcribe the focus group into text,

DOI: 10.4324/9781003031161-5

you have raw data. If you refine that data by identifying patterns of reasons people give for buying season tickets, you have information. Information is descriptive but does not yield much in terms of insights. If you analyze the themes to determine the relevance of each them to your team, you have knowledge. The analysis allows you to interpret the information and convert it into knowledge that can guide decisions about season tickets and how to promote them. Interpretation converts information into knowledge and knowledge helps managers make decisions. Interpreting information is a two-step process. The first step is determining whether or not the information is relevant to the organization. The second step is classifying the information as threat or opportunity. A threat can hurt the organization while an opportunity can benefit an organization. We will elaborate on threat and opportunity in the next section. Scanning is simply a starting point. It says, "Hey, this is something we should look at more closely."

Obviously, every organization has a broad internal and external environment to scan. Scanning is often described as looking for trends or issues that could affect the organization. An example would be an online retailer being concerned about Congressional interest in taxing online purchases or a food manufacturer interested in potential new labeling requirements being discussed by the Food and Drug Administration. One way to give more direction to scanning is to think about it in terms of stakeholders.

Stakeholders are those people that can influence and are influenced by your organization (Freeman, 1984). The two earlier examples were governmental. Governmental decisions can have a significant impact on how an organization operates and its ability to generate revenue. Changes in consumers can affect organizations. If consumer tastes can shift, some products and service will increase in demand while others will fade. But consumer values can change as well. Consider how over the past two decades there is a growing interest among consumers about social responsibility and sustainability. Organizations have had to adapt to these demands by becoming more socially responsible and valuing sustainability. The Cleveland Major League Baseball team power their stadium from 100 percent renewable wind energy. AAMI Park stadium in Melbourne, Australia collects rainwater for use in the stadium saving 500,000 gallons of water per year. Each of these sustainability efforts was informed understanding the way stakeholders now value sustainability. Major League Soccer in the US created special Earth Day shirts made from ocean plastics. These are just three examples of how scanning can be built around your stakeholders. You can scan for information relevant to or created by your key stakeholders.

Here is a list of common stakeholders:

Customers
Employees
Investors/Shareholders
Suppliers
Government

Competitors
News Media
Community
Creditors
Unions
Activist Groups and Non-governmental Organizations
*Stakeholders share an interest in the organization. This is a very broad way of segmenting your possible audience into more meaningful groups.

Social listening is an example of scanning. Social listening involves collecting and analyzing select social media platforms for direct mentions of an organization or its brands, customer feedback, or discussions of specific keywords related to your organization, brand, competitors, or industry. Note how social media requires analysis of the data not just collected a lot of words or images. Social listening adds value by providing insights, not by simply collecting massive amounts of data. Social listening is an extension of the older idea of media monitoring which originally tracked traditional media coverage but has since expanded to include social media platforms. Social listening is a direct result of the robust digital environment that surrounds sport. HubSpot, Social Sprout, and Hootsuite all provide services for social listening that covers a range of platforms and then translates the data into a dashboard that helps managers to interpret the information—to locate threats and opportunities.

The digital environment makes scanning easier and more complicated. Scanning is easier because information can be accessed so readily. There are any number of studies conducted in industry and academics that have documented the way consumers and employees are embracing sustainability and social responsibility. The 2019 Retail and Sustainability Survey by CGS found that 68 percent of consumers said that product sustainability was important to their purchasing decision. And 35 percent said they would pay 25 percent more for a product that was sustainable (CGS, 2019). Moreover, the data consistently find that younger consumers value sustainability much more than older consumers (Makower, 2020). Younger employees expect their employers to be concerned about sustainability and even would work for less money to be at an organization that was sustainable (Peters, 2019). This information on changing consumer and employee values is easy to find on the Internet. Similarly, there is no problem finding out what activists are interested in and if that might relate to your organization. Major activist groups have highly informative web sites and social media feeds with potentially valuable information.

The complicating factor is the sheer amount of information. You are more likely to suffer from information overload when scanning than struggle to find information. Artificial intelligence (AI) is one method of sifting through vast amounts of information, what some term "big data." Most social listening and media monitoring are a basic form of AI that uses computer programs to content analyze messages the words in messages. More advanced AI algorithms can code messages (text and visuals) for themes and message frames. However, the use of AI should be coupled with human intelligence (HI). People need to review the AI results to determine the accuracy and relevance on the information being collected and summarized (Reese, 2017). A critical aspect of the HI review of scanning results is determining the relevance of the information to the organization and the nature of that relevance—is the information an indicator of a threat or an opportunity?

SWOT, TOWS, and PEST Analyses: Techniques for Analyzing Scanning Data

It should be clear by now that scanning is not random but should be organized. So how do you organize scanning? That is a fair question. This section provides three different tools that people have been using in organizations for a long period of time. Each offers some insight into what you are scanning for and how you might assess the information you collect through scanning.

SWOT

SWOT stands for strengths, weaknesses, opportunities, and threats. It is a tool commonly used to help develop strategy for organizations. SWOT is important because it provides meaning to the terms opportunity and threats and offers a systematic approach to this assessment. Strengths and weaknesses are internal to the organization, the internal environment. Opportunities and threats are external to the organization, the external environment. Strengths are what an organization does well. How are you better than other entities you would consider your competition? For example, do you have better quality services or are you more agile at making changes. Strengths are your assets. Weaknesses are things you could do better. These are points where your competition is currently better than you are. Perhaps you have a weak reputation meaning stakeholders really do not think much about your organization or you lack a strong social media presence. Weaknesses are your liabilities. Your job is to capitalize on and maintain your strengths while seeking to reduce your weaknesses (Gürel & Tat, 2017).

Opportunities and threats are more external to the organization but are linked to your strengths and weaknesses. Opportunities are chances to do something positive for an organization such as enhance the organizational reputation or improve employee morale. Managers need to think about how they can use strengths to leverage opportunities. Threats are dangers to the organization that could negatively impact the organization. Threats could be a competitor's new product that decreases your market share or a new regulation that could hinder the ability of your organization to operate effectively. Managers should try to understand how your weaknesses might expose the organization to threats. For instance, your lack of a strong social media presence might result in competitors using their social media savvy to lure

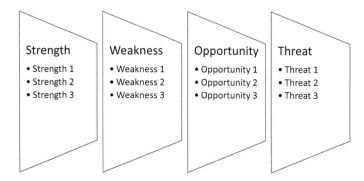

Figure 4.1 SWOT analysis recording format.

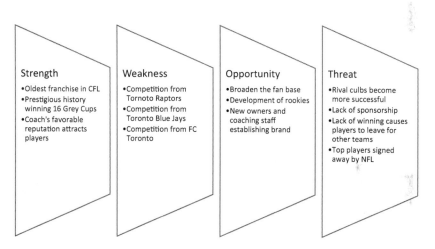

Figure 4.2 Sample SWOT analysis.
This is a sample SWOT analysis conducted by Suth Speaks Sport (2017) for the Toronto Argonauts.

stakeholders away from your organization. Figure 4.1 presents an example of how to record information created in the SWAT analysis. Figure 4.2 offers a sample SWOT analysis for the Toronto Argonauts of the Canadian Football League (CFL).

TOWS

TOWS looks like a simple rearrangement of the letters in SWOT. Yes, the same four words are used but TOWS is designed to help you see how threats, opportunities, weaknesses, and strengths become converted into strategy— serve to guide your decisions and actions. The TOWS process starts with four

External	External	Internal	Internal
Opportunities (O)	Threats (T)	Strengths (S)	Weaknesses (W)
1.	1.	1.	1.
2.	2.	2.	2.
3.	3.	3.	3.
4.	4.	4.	4.

Figure 4.3 TOWS matrix.

questions: (1) How do you make the most of your strengths? (2) How do you circumvent weaknesses? (3) How do you capitalize on opportunities? (4) How do you manage threats? Managers use the TOWS matrix presented in Figure 4.3 to guide their thinking about these questions. You then combine the four factors to develop one of four different strategies:

> SO Strategy: strengths are used to maximize opportunities
> ST Strategy: strengths are used to minimize threats
> WO Strategy: minimize weaknesses to take advantage of opportunities
> WT Strategy: minimize weaknesses to avoid threats (Weihrich, 1982)

With the strengths and opportunities (SO) strategy, you focus on how your strengths can be used to leverage opportunities. The strengths and threats (ST) strategy seeks to employ your strengths to avoid threats. The weakness and opportunities (WO) strategy serves to use opportunities to overcome a weakness. The weakness and threats (WT) strategy tries to minimize weaknesses as a way to avoid threats. The WT is a very defensive strategy and seeks to avoid loss rather than to create any gains. TOWS is just a more direct way of translating threats, opportunities, weaknesses, and threats into action (strategy).

PEST

PEST is a process for thinking about threats. PEST stands for political, economic, socio-cultural, and technological. These represent four broad categories of threats and present a way to organize how you are thinking about threats. Political centers on how government can affect your organizations. Governments can be local, state (regional), or national. Organizations that operate in multiple locations and multiple countries have a much more complicated set of political threats to consider. Changes in state laws in the U.S. have had significant implication for sports gambling which does impact leagues and teams. New York state, for instance, had a period of time where it banned online betting for fantasy sports. When that ban was lifted, the decision affected not only companies such as FanDuel and DraftKings that run fantasy sports betting but had implications for professional teams as the role on online sports betting expanded as well. Economic considers how factors such as employment rates, national economic growth or decline, and amount of disposal income of stakeholders. An economic downturn can reduce disposal income meaning less spending on a sport. Social-cultural include changing age patterns, shifts in values, and the varying importance of social issues such as equal pay and same-sex marriage. Leagues and teams need to address issues of pay equality when there are similar leagues for women and men. Technological seeks to understand how new technologies can change your industry and how stakeholder use of technology changes demands on your organization. Consider how Major League Baseball demanded all their stadiums supply Wi-Fi because fans want to be able to access and to use Wi-Fi while they are at sporting events. PEST is simply one way to organize your discussion of potential threats (Sammut-Bonnici & Galea, 2015).

At this point, we should talk about likelihood and impact. Likelihood and impact are two criteria that are used to assess both threats and opportunities. Likelihood are the odds that a specific threat or opportunity is likely to emerge. Impact is the potential negative effect of a threat or positive effect of an opportunity on an organization. As a team, you should try to assign a value to each threat and opportunity you find. Typically threats and opportunities are rated from 1 to 10 with 1 being the 1 being the weakest and 10 being the strongest score. If you assign likelihood and impact scores to threats and opportunities, it becomes easy to compare them and to determine which threats or opportunities warrant further attention. We will return to the idea of ranking threats and opportunities in the discussion of deliverables.

Monitoring

Not everything you find when you are scanning needs your immediate attention. There are times when something seems to have potential but just does not have enough salience to demand your attention. Yet you do not want to ignore something you think could become important. That is where monitoring comes into play. Monitoring is when you watch something closely. If the situation begins increasing in salience, you will be ready to then take action. Media monitoring is a perfect example. Media monitoring companies provide updated information about how people are talking about your organization or a specific concern in digital and traditional channels. For instance, how do people talk about your team or their in-game experiences? The analysis is close to real time so you will know quickly if there are shifts in discussions that could increase the salience of the situation. Kangaroo leather is a real example of monitoring in sport. You might be monitoring how people feel about the use of kangaroo leather in your soccer cleats if you work for a major athletic shoe company or a soccer team. You know a small group of people have been talking about the concern for years due to mistreatment of kangaroos in the process. However, the issue seems to be limited to a small group of like-minded stakeholders. The monitoring would show how this small network of people were talking about the concern. Monitoring would alert you if suddenly other people began to discuss and to share the concern with a wider number of people. You visually could see the change in the data as the small network of people began to grow into a much larger network. Figure 4.4 is a hypothetic representation of the shift in the discussion of kangaroo leather in soccer cleats. You engage in monitoring when you find a concern that could be important to the organization if it increases in salience. Monitoring allows you to determine if or when that shift in salience occurs.

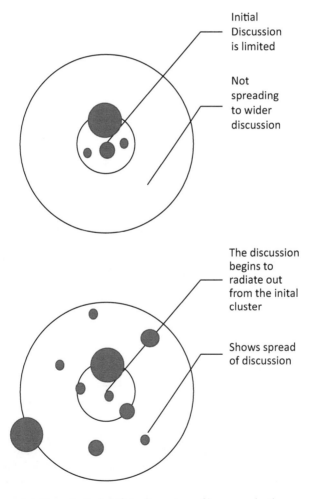

Figure 4.4 Hypothetical shift in discussion of kangaroo leather.

Deliverables from Scanning and Monitoring

Deliverables are what you create during the strategic communication process. At each step in the strategic communication process there are specific deliverables that you should have created. For scanning and monitoring, the deliverables are lists. The first list you create are the concerns you have identified from your scanning including your SWOT and TOWS analyses. This is a running list because you will update it with the opportunities and threats you have identified now and ones you will add in the future. The second list is your tentative prioritization of the concerns. This is your initial assessment of the opportunities and threats and is based upon the likelihood and impact scores you have assigned to each threat and opportunity. The prioritization list represents those concerns that warrant further attention (seem the most salient), those you will monitor, and those you will discard. Table 4.1 offers a simple format for your tentative prioritization list. Notice the table includes a space for a short explanation of each assessment you made. It is important to indicate why each concern received a particular categorization. The prioritization is tentative because during the research, the next step, the information you uncover might result in a modification of the prioritization.

Running Example: Opportunity for Watford FC

For our running example of an opportunity, we will be using the British football club Watford. Watford is a small-market team that seeks to be competitive in order to retain its position in the Premier League. (Watford was relegated to the Championship in 2020 but will return to the Premier League in 2021. This opportunity began when Watford was in the Premier League, hence we will reference them as a Premier League team in the running example of opportunity.) In the Premier League, each year the bottom three teams are dropped down to the next lower level in football while three teams are promoted from the Championship. Being in the Premier League adds over $200 million to a team's revenue due mostly to the broadcast rights associated with the Premier League. Teams such as Watford are always looking for ways to build fan support for the team.

Watford receives information from the Premier League office about a program to encourage teams to provide sensory rooms for fans. Sensory

Table 4.1 Sample prioritization of concerns (threats and opportunities)

Item Prioritization	Likelihood	Impact	Total
End of sponsorship deal (T or O)	9	8	17
Decline in game attendance (T)	5	9	14
Use of TikTok platform (O)	10	2	12
Injury to key player(s) (T)	6	4	10
Signing of new player(s) (O)	5	4	9

rooms are calm spaces that allow people with the autism spectrum disorder (ASD) and similar conditions to enjoy a match. Many people with ASD are overwhelmed by the sights and sounds of a football match resulting in their inability to attend matches. The Premier League is willing to help provide funding for sensory rooms along with financial support from the BT Disability Programme and the disability sports charity the Lord's Taverners. The goal of the program is to help make sport more inclusive by allowing those with ASD to share the match-day experience (Sensory, 2016). The team has also received a letter from long-time Watford fan lamenting how her seven-year old son with ASD has tried attending games but had to leave when he became overwhelmed by the experience. She was hoping the team could find a way to help families in her situation by providing a special viewing area for ASD fans.

The strategic communication identifies the creation of a sensory room as an opportunity. The costs associated with creating the sensory room will be minimal because of the funding provided by the Premier League and the charities. The percentage of fans utilizing the sensory room will be rather small meaning the opportunity is not directly related to revenue. Rather, the opportunity involves social evaluation. Fan inclusion is a form of corporate social responsibility (CSR) for a soccer team. CSR is an important driver from organizational reputations. The Reputation Institute reports that over 40 percent of an organization's reputation is derived from CSR (Smith, 2012). Watford could enhance its reputation (create a social assessment asset) by constructing and proving a sensor room for its fans. Some fans and the community in general could be impressed by Watford's commitment to those with ASD. Because ASD is frequently associated with children, the sensory room will be considered family friendly. Family friendly is important because "family" is a central element of Watford's organizational identity. The opportunity is giving a 10 for likelihood and a 5 for impact. Likelihood is a 10 because a few other teams have already created sensor rooms as part of the larger Premier League effort. That means building the sensory is very likely with the support from other sources. The impact is a 5 because only certain segments of fans and the community will be interested in the concerns related to those with ASD. However, the sensory room with resonate with many stakeholders (fans and community members) attracted to the family aspect of the team's identity.

Running Example: Threat for the Los Angeles Dodgers

For our running example, threat, we will be using the Major League Baseball (MLB) team the Los Angeles Dodgers. The Los Angeles Dodgers are a prominent professional U.S. baseball team with a long and storied history including a number of World Series titles as the best team in MLB. The Los Angeles Dodgers were originally the Brooklyn Dodgers before the team moved in 1958. The Brooklyn Dodgers integrated when Jackie Robinson took the field for the team on April 15, 1947. Prior to this day, U.S. baseball was segregated with African Americans only playing in the Negro leagues and MLB reserved for white players.

On June 6, 2020, it is estimated that over half a million people in 550 locations across the U.S. joined anti-racism protests fueled by the video George Floyd being killed by police with a knee on his neck in Minneapolis, MN. The protests became associated with Black Lives Matter, and organization and social movement that began in 2013 (Buchanan, Bui, & Patel, 2020). The protests created pressure on organizations to speak out about systemic racism that exists within the U.S. Public opinion polls clearly showed people expected organizations to address the topic of racisms (Parker, Horowitz, & Anderson, 2020). The need to address racism appeared on the scanning of every organization in the U.S., including sports teams, as a possible threat. The need to speak about systemic racism is a threat because not speaking about the topic could harm the organization's social approvals and perhaps sales of products and services. The financial danger was reinforced by polling data indicating people were willing to boycott organizations that remained silent (Murphy, 2020). Threat is a dual-sided concept. Ignoring or mishandling a threat creates a downside for an organization while effective handling of a threat creates an upside (Churning, 2020). Like every other sports team in the U.S., the Los Angeles Dodgers' strategic communication team identified the need to speak about systemic racism as a threat.

References

Buchanan, L., Biu, Q., & Patel, J.K. (2020, July 3). Black Lives Matter may be the largest movement in U.S. history, *The New York Times*. Retrieved from https://www.nytimes.com/interactive/2020/07/03/us/george-floyd-protests-crowd-size.html

Churning, The (2020, April 15). Opportunities and threats do not exist, The Churning. Retrieved from http://www.thechurning.net/opportunities-and-threats-do-not-exist/

CGS (2019). GS Survey Reveals 'Sustainability' Is Driving Demand and Customer Loyalty, CGS. Retrieved from https://www.cgsinc.com/en/infographics/CGS-Survey-Reveals-Is-Driving-Demand-and-Customer-Loyalty

Freeman, R. E. 1984. *Strategic management: A stakeholder approach*. Boston: Pitman Publishing.

Gürel, E., and M. Tat. 2017. SWOT analysis: a theoretical review. *Journal of International Social Research*, 10(51), 994–1006.

Makower, J. (2020). Earth Day and the polling of America, 2020. Retrieved from https://www.greenbiz.com/article/earth-day-and-polling-america-2020.

Murphy, C. (2020). Boycott for Black Lives: People plan to stop spending in companies to don't support BLM, *USA Today*. Retrieved from https://eu.usatoday.com/story/money/2020/06/18/boycotts-people-plan-stop-spending-stores-dont-support-blm/3208170001/

Parker, K., Horowitz, J., & Anderson, M. (2020, June 12). Amid protests, majorities across racial and ethnic groups express support of Black Lives Matter Movement, Pew Research Center. Retrieved from https://www.pewresearch.org/social-trends/2020/06/12/amid-protests-majorities-across-racial-and-ethnic-groups-express-support-for-the-black-lives-matter-movement/

Pecánek, M. (2020, August 13). What is share of voice? How to measure it across channels, Ahrefs. Retrieved from https://ahrefs.com/blog/share-of-voice/#:~:text=You%20monitor%20keywords%20(brand%20names,to%20the%20overall%20market%20mentions.

Peters, A. (2019). Most millennials would take a pay cut to work at an environmentally responsible company. Retrieved from https://www.fastcompany.com/90306556/most-millennials-would-take-a-pay-cut-to-work-at-a-sustainable-company.

Reese, H. (2017, February 23). Understanding the differences between AI, machine learning, and deep learning, TechRepublic. Retrieved from https://www.techrepublic.com/article/understanding-the-differences-between-ai-machine-learning-and-deep-learning/

Sammut-Bonnici, T., & Galea, D. (2015). PEST analysis. In C. L. Cooper (Ed.), *Wiley Encylopedia of Management* (Volume 12). Wiley Online Library. https://blogs.napier.ac.uk/docman/wp-content/uploads/sites/54/2020/01/PEST.pdf

Sensory rooms will make a difference (2016, October 18). Premier League. Retrieved from https://www.premierleague.com/news/123426

Smith, J. (2012). The companies with the best CSR reputations. Retrieved from www.forbes.com/sites/jacquelynsmith/2012/12/10/the-companies-with-the-best-csr-reputations/

Suth, T. (2017, December 15). Toronto Argonauts brand analysis, Suth Speaks Sport. Retrieved from https://suthspeakssport.weebly.com/cfl/toronto-argonauts-brand-analysis

Weihrich, H. (1982). The TOWS matrix—A tool for situational analysis. *Long Range Planning, 15*(2), 54–66.

5 Researching and Refining Opportunities and Threats

Once strategic communicators find possible opportunities and threats, additional research is needed to determine which opportunities to pursue and which threats require attention. To make such decisions, additional research is required. Strategic communicators need to feel they have enough information for making an informed decision, what is often called situational awareness.

Situational awareness requires research. Research is a way to collect more data from the environment to understand the nature of the situation the strategic communicator is facing. Research is defined as "the systematic investigation into and study of materials and sources in order to establish facts and reach new conclusions." The research required to develop a successful strategic sport communication campaign also requires the systematic study of materials and sources. Materials include secondary—or already existing—artifacts such as news articles or scientific reports. Sources are, for example, any person involved in the topic at hand, which includes people who work in sport, the end user or sports fan, and even the target audience. This chapter will review the research methods typically employed to research or study materials and sources to help the strategic communicator to establish facts and reach new conclusions for the development of a strategic sport communication campaign.

Secondary Data Sources

It is important to first understand the difference between secondary data sources and primary data collection. The differences between the two are: what information already exists and what information the strategic communicator will create. To explain, secondary data sources consists of the information that already exists, such as reports or news articles created by other researchers and authors. Secondary data sources are imperative to first explore when embarking on any strategic sport communication campaign creation because it helps to situate our own unique and new research efforts on which to build the campaign. For example, we might need to know how much Nike, on average, pays for each athlete-level endorsement before we suggest such an endorsement for our own client. Or, we might want to read

DOI: 10.4324/9781003031161-6

an annual report regarding the state of sport consumerism in a particular country before expanding a line of merchandise to that country. Secondary data sources are someone else's primary data that was collected and now provides foundational knowledge strategic communicators can build upon without having to "reinvent the wheel." So, if the secondary data revealed there is market opportunity to expand to another country, then the next step would be to build upon that already existing knowledge and dig deeper by collecting the specific primary data for the exact market segment profitable for the client. In this section, we pause to discuss the secondary data sources communicators can explore when embarking on the research necessary to for the development of a strategic sport communication campaign.

University libraries and other online databases are rich resources from which to mine secondary data. Seeking out secondary data aids a strategic communicator in positioning an argument, gathering industry-level facts, and exploring the economical or sociological big-picture aspects necessary to consider when developing a campaign. Digital repositories like Redbooks, ProQuest, or Statista offer access to literally millions of statistics and other vital information. Typically, secondary data was someone else's primary data collection process that is now available for others to use as a Launchpad for their own work.

Secondary data is imperative to the creation and development of a strategic communication campaign. This is because the communicator can learn the baseline considerations for shaping the campaign. These underlying considerations include important planning aspects such as identifying target audiences, budget planning, media buys, and the transmedia communication channels that will best help the campaign flow where it needs to flow to achieve the desired goals and objectives. In other words, secondary data are the positional sources for an emerging campaign.

The following overarching topics are the best places to begin with secondary data:

1. *Fans.* Strategic sport communication campaigns are built to reach or recruit fans. No campaign can become successful without first identifying exactly who you need to reach. Secondary data can help a researcher identify who their client's current fans are as well as those fans' baseline demographic information. More importantly, secondary data can help a researcher identify who *are not* your client's fans but should be. Secondary data can offer widespread insight into virtually every consumption detail of interest to campaign consumption in relation to sports fans. *Sources include*: Statista, Forbes, Census.gov.

2. *Traditional Media.* Traditional media include newspapers, magazines, television and radio broadcasts, and other media sources. Traditional media report on sports and these reports can provide a rich data source for shaping new campaign and assessing the success or failures of past campaigns. Traditional media typically feature sport-specific sections. A deeper discussion on researching traditional media sources as a primary data source can be

found in the quantitative methods section that follows later in this chapter. *Sources include*: ProQuest, *New York Times*.

3. *Social Media*. Social media allows strategic communicators the opportunity to participate in social listening. Social listening and observation of social media use are rich sources of secondary data for campaign creation. Social listening reveals how consumers respond, what interests them enough to respond, and where they are and are active throughout social media channels. Strategic communicators focused on a transmedia campaign should regularly participate in secondary data collection through social listening, scanning and monitoring. *Sources include*: Hootsuite.

4. *Critics*. If all we ever do is talk with our friends, followers, and cheerleaders, we would never come to realize the truths about the world that surrounds us. Critics are a rich source of secondary data because the picture they paint is not always rosy but instead provides food for thought. A critic's job is to poke holes in the topic at hand. Those holes reveal weak spots, which should be of high concern to any campaign strategist. It is recommended to review critiques regarding your client and all competitors before embarking on primary data collection. *Sources include*: Opinion/Editorials, *New York Times*.

Collecting Primary Data

Once a strategic communicator has acquired base knowledge from already existing secondary data sources, the primary data collection process can begin. Collecting primary data allows a strategic communicator to investigate the niche foci that will best benefit the strategic sport communication campaign—whether the aim is to find an opportunity or to solve or deter a particular threat. It is not enough to know a person is an NBA fan, we must also know which team that fan follows most, the level of that person's fanship, and which NBA official merchandise s/he is most likely to purchase. None of this information can be gleamed from a secondary source. This information requires primary data collection from the primary source: the NBA fan.

Primary data collection should be driven by the specific problem the strategic communicator seeks to solve. Using the NBA example, a problem solver might seek answers regarding how best to market a new line of player jerseys to women. Secondary data sources informed the strategic communicator that 28 percent of all sales in the last quarter were purchases made by women but the NBA wishes to increase these sales by 10 percent by the end of the fiscal year. It is not enough to know that 28 percent of all sales last quarter were purchases by women. The secondary data source was informative enough to know how current sales are broken down by sex, and it helps to identify a baseline and set a goal, but this is not enough information to create the specific strategic plan for a campaign to raise the percentage of sales to women. So, what would be the next step? The next step would be to gather primary data straight from the source: women.

Primary data collection from sources, such as the women mentioned in the NBA example, involves capturing or measuring an individual's beliefs, attitudes, intentions, and behaviors. One pre-consideration for such data collection is the categorization of your aim: *Are you investigating a psychological or a sociological aspect of sport?* In general terms, a comprehensive campaign would include both. Both psychological and sociological interests connect to each the beliefs, attitudes, intentions, and behaviors to differing degrees. Some are obvious: attitude is connected to the psychological and behavior is connected to the sociological—but both can connect inversely, as well. Just being aware of these categories is critical to being successful in gathering and interpreting primary data. Knowing at the onset by parsing out your problem-solving approach in these two, overarching areas of the human experience will pay-off in the end because, as discussed in Chapter 3, fan behaviors encompass both the psychological antecedents and the resultant sociological behavior of sports fans.

Qualitative and Quantitative Research Methods

A researcher should understand that data are categorized under two main umbrellas: qualitative and quantitative. One easy way to remember these two types of data categorizations is by thinking about the words themselves: "qual" meaning quality and "quant" meaning quantity. The quality or qualitative approach can be thought of as the lived experience. Qualitative research allows researchers to dig deep in the human experience. Quantity or quantitative research allows a research to quantify the human experience by generalizing more broadly and collecting a quantity of experiences. Each category or type of data have their strengths and weaknesses. Each also can solve its own set of problems or explore, to differing degrees, questions that must be answered to form or inform a strategic sport communication campaign.

Whether you choose a qualitative or quantitative focus, primary data collection efforts in communication-related studies generally include the following methods:

Archival Sources: Libraries and Databases
Qualitative Methods: Interviews, Focus Groups, and Observation
Quantitative Methods: Content Analysis, Experiments, and Surveys

A research method is the process used to collect data. A method is a set of uniform practices. For example, when conducting qualitative methods, which include in-depth interviews, focus groups or observational research, you are studying the psychological and sociological behaviors of humans and their lived experiences. The method of interviewing includes speaking with someone at length (or in-depth) and recording their responses and reactions to your semi-structured set of questions. If in-depth interviews are your method of choice, then you will follow the same process and use the same questionnaire with each participant you interview. The same is true regarding quantitative methods, which include content analysis, experiments, and surveys.

Qualitative Methods of Data Collection

Archival Sources

Archival sources are rich deposits of information. One reason for its richness is because, as the old adage notes, those who do not learn from history are doomed to repeat it. Archival information can provide insight into the norms and occurrences that have happened up to this point in time in relation to sports, sport consumption, sport consumerism, sports leagues, sports teams, athletes, and so much more. University libraries are especially rich sources for archival sources. For example, university libraries have a catalog of databases that students can access, which includes both physical materials and digital repositories. Historical collections are rich resources for historical, critical culture, and rhetorical primary data.

Interviews, Focus Groups, and Observation

Interviews, focus groups, and observations are all qualitative data collection methods. These methods allow a researcher to embed themselves with target audience members and dig deep into the experiences and behaviors of current or potential consumers. A researcher can thus qualitatively research the human experience by asking probing questions or observing certain behaviors. Data, in these instances, are the words and phrases collected in conversation or the behaviors observed. Once the data is collected, researchers analyze the data by conducting a thematic analysis of the collected data. Thematic analyses will be discussed in more detail at the end of this section. First, let's review each of these qualitative methods one by one.

In-depth Interviews

In-depth interviews are best described as a semi-structured question-and-answer session between an interviewer and an interviewee, usually a consumer. An interviewer should enter the interview with a semi-structured questionnaire to ask about the most important matters the researcher wishes to learn. A great interview becomes conversational yet is still probing for answers to specific questions. To explain, the researcher should begin with a list of specific questions, also known as a semi-structured questionnaire, and allow the interviewee to answer in as much length and detail as they wish in response to each question. This rich data—the answers to the researcher's questions—can become further defined when the interviewee expands on the topic at hand by mentioning a facet of the topic that the researcher hadn't considered in structuring the original questionnaire. It is always best practice toward the end of an interview to ask the interviewee if they have anything to add to the overall topic or if you were remiss in asking a particularly important question. Oftentimes, interviewees will share insight that the interviewer had not yet thought to ask.

The researcher conducting an in-depth interview will repeat the process of interviewing individuals until saturation is achieved. Saturation is achieved when interviewees begin to offer the same or similar answers as other interviewees. Once saturation is achieved, the researcher has collected enough data. The data that will be analyzed from this method include the words and phrases the interviewees used in their responses to the semi-structured questionnaire, as well as any behavioral reactions to those questions. Qualitative data analysis will be discussed at the end of this section.

Focus Groups

A focus group is a group of consumers who gather in a room with an interviewer to focus on the topic being researched. Focus groups are conversational, open discussions where consumers express their beliefs, attitudes, intentions, and behavior regarding some sort of an exchange or experience with the research topic at hand; oftentimes a specific product or narrowed topic of discussion. Researchers should select a diverse group of individuals to participate in a focus group for the widest range of perceptions and preferences to be shared.

A good focus group interviewer allows for deep debate among the participants regarding the topic at hand but stops the group short of any argumentative or insulting speech directed toward each other or others. A group of students once held a focus group to conduct research for a new Black-focused news organization in West Virginia. Participants explained that they feel the state lacks Black influencers. This was data the team could research further to integrate into their strategic communication plan for their client and make recommendations regarding how the new news service could provide a digital platform for Black influencers throughout the state of West Virginia.

The focus group meets in a room all at the same time while the interviewer guides the conversations and presents the questions. Focus groups should be recorded; both video and audio are recommended, with consent from those participating. The recording should later be transcribed verbatim for thematic analysis. This can be a time-consuming task, so be certain to plan accordingly. It is also best to have a second researcher present to observe the focus group and take notes regarding the mannerisms and voice inflictions of the participants, which will only enrich your newly collected dataset.

Observational Research

Observational research is conducted by inserting the researcher into the situation being researched so that the researcher can observe how others

participate in that particular experience. It is important to go into an observation with an open mind and a blank notebook. Field notes are the deliverable data of observational research. The researcher should detail how people
react to the setting, including what they wear, the things they say, where they
roam, and how they might display emotion.

Observational research is helpful in numerous ways. Strategic
communicators can personally observe actual, real-time interactions.
Observing consumers interacting with the product or campaign at hand can
uncover both opportunities and threats, and informs communicators and
campaign creators how best to work out the kinks or enhance certain aspects
of interactivity or engagement.

For example, a group of students once attended a football game when
researching an emerging sports league. They observed who attended the
game, how those in attendance interacted with the game and with other
attendees, and how the league and teams hosted the game. This was an especially rich observational opportunity since the newly emerged league was
still defining its image and live game experience. The observational research
experience additionally built-up these students' own identification with
their project. They reported that this observational research experience
enabled them to better construct their team's survey questions and finalize
their target audience demographics for their strategic sport communication
campaign.

These qualitative research methods result in rich psychological and sociological data regarding the human experience. These data represent actual
interactivity or engagement, and these data reveal consumers' beliefs,
attitudes, intentions, and behavior. Once the data has been collected, it is
the strategic communicator's job to analyze the data. Data analysis should be
conducted in such a way that the process organizes the data in a consistent
and coherent manner to allow the data to tell the story. Thematic analysis is
the most common process applied to analyzing qualitative data.

Thematic Analysis

If you interviewed five people and three of them said the same or similar
thing in response to a question, congratulations! You have an emergent
theme in your qualitative data.

If you conducted the interviews and/or transcribed the interviews, you
are likely to be familiar with your data already. If someone else completed
these tasks, it is important to read through all responses before attempting
the thematic analysis. Having broad knowledge of the overall data set will
in thinking broadly throughout the process. Once familiar with the data,
the researcher will code the data. This can be as simple as assigning letters
or numbers to topics. For example, if gender is an important considered
mentioned in several interviews, a particular number or letter is assigned to
every paragraph or sentence that mentions gender throughout the transcripts.

You will continue this process until all topics have been exhausted. Which themes are most often present? Which are most often discussed in response to particular questions asked?

It is standard practice to present three emergent themes from qualitative data. Researchers may end up with more than three themes or with fewer than three. It is important not to force this process but to rather allow the process to be either inductive or deductive, depending upon the problem the researcher is seeking to solve. To explain, inductive interpretation of the data will enable the researcher to allow the responses to fully create the themes. Alternatively, deductive analysis categorizes the themes and assesses how many responses fall into those themed categories. Either approach is valuable to a strategic sport communication campaign.

Software: MAXQDA or NVivo is commonly used for qualitative data analysis.

Deliverables

> In-Depth Interview: Semi-structured Questionnaire, Transcription, Thematic Analysis
> Focus Group: Focus Group Guide, Transcription, Thematic Analysis
> Observation: Detailed Field Notes, Thematic Analysis

Pro tip: Journalists are trained not simply to ask yes/no questions but to ask open-ended questions in order to receive richer responses for quotes in news articles. As researchers collecting new data, take this concept one step further and ask yourself if your question is open-ended enough to elicit a variety of answers; answers from which themes could emerge. For example, it is not enough to ask a respondent whether or not they are a sports fan (a yes/no question). Instead, ask them what makes them a sports fan (open-ended question). You might further probe by asking them to describe how or in what ways others might describe their behavior as a sports fan. Themes that might emerge in response to these questions could include: regularly watching games on TV, wearing sports team logos on clothing, and sharing about sports on social media.

Quantitative Methods of Data Collection

Quantitative methods differ from qualitative methods by quantifying the human experience instead of documenting the in-depth, personalized qualitative experiences of individuals. Quantitative methods help to answer research questions and hypotheses in a broader scope. Research questions and hypotheses aid the researcher in achieving the specific aim of the research being conducted or aids in identifying, defining, or solving a problem. This section provides a broad overview regarding the key concepts to consider when designing a quantitative research method, and reviews the most common quantitative research methods in strategic sport communication: surveys, content analysis, and social network analysis.

Quantitative methods allow a researcher to collect larger datasets so that they can more broadly generalize the results of the survey. Recall here that both qualitative and quantitative research are primary data collection methods that build upon the initial, secondary data research. That secondary data research should then inform a campaign creator of the various consumer demographics of interest. Once the population of interest is identified, a quantitative researcher will need to determine a representative sample. Sampling a population means research is conducted only on a portion of the overall population. Sampling is necessary in survey research because it is often not realistic to survey *all* people in a target demographic, which is termed a census. Think for a moment, would you be able to reach every soccer fan in England? Probably not, but you could reach a representative sample of soccer fans in England. Sample size is dependent upon the particular population Sampling requires a lot of preplanning because a sampling frame and a sensible sampling strategy to reach that sampling frame are key to being successful with quantitative research.

A sampling frame can be random or nonrandom. Random sampling means that anyone within the specified population has an equal chance of being selected to participate. This would mean that any individual who resides in England has an equal chance of being selected to participate in the survey. Nonrandom means the selection is purposeful. To make the England residents sample nonrandom, the researcher would specify that a survey respondent must be an England resident who self-identifies as a fan of soccer and has attended at least one soccer match within the past year. In the nonrandom scenario, the sampling frame is much more specific and therefore less random. Once a sampling frame is decided, a similar sampling strategy should be selected to reach members of the random or nonrandom sample.

Sampling strategies are similarly conceptualized as sampling frames. Sampling strategies are based upon probability or nonprobability. A probability sampling strategy has a known nonzero chance of inclusion. Techniques for collecting a probability sample include the simple random, systematic, stratified, cluster, or area techniques. For example, cluster sampling would divide all possible respondents into two clusters: Manchester City or Manchester United fans. So, the researcher would randomly sample from each cluster of those two teams' fans.

A nonprobability sampling strategy depends upon personal judgment. This type of sampling is dependent upon the research purpose. Nonprobability sampling techniques include convenience, judgment, snowball, and quota (see Box 5.1). The most common applied research method for an undergraduate survey research project is the snowball method. The snowball method is explained as a snowball being rolled around until it becomes large enough from the extra-accumulated snow to become the base of a snowman. If you are delivering an online survey, the snowball method is an economical way to reach respondents by posting about the survey on social media and then asking friends to share your announcement. As social media users continue to share the announcement, the online survey accumulates more and more respondents.

Once the sampling frame and sampling method are determined, researchers also need to spend time operationalizing exactly what must be defined, collected, and measured through the primary data collection process.

BOX 5.1 Nonprobability sampling techniques

Convenience: *proximity equals a quick stop*

A Convenience sample is conveniently accessed by the researcher. For example, students interview fellow students on campus. Due to the close proximity, this sample of respondents is easily, or conveniently, accessed.

Judgment: *ask the "experts"*

A Judgment sample, also called a purposive sample, is chosen when a specific set of parameters would be best regarding respondents and their specific set of qualifiers. For example, selecting specific experts on a topic of research might provide the best data for your project. The term "expert" here is used loosely. A researcher might be purposive to survey only Arizona Cardinals football team fans regarding "die-hard" fanship of a team that has never enjoyed a winning season by winning a Super Bowl.

Snowball: *recruit friends, grow your sample*

The Snowball technique often utilizes personal networks (both online and offline). Think of a snowball rolling down a hill, collecting snow and growing larger as it rolls. A researcher might share an online survey through social media platforms and ask their friends and family members to share the information with their networks and so on.

Quota: *set a limit, reach the limit*

A Quota sampling technique is defined as setting and reaching a specified goal. Demographic quotas are often important quotas to set for sport-related research. For example, ensuring ample and diverse responses regarding race/ethnicity demographics for research regarding social justice issues in sport is imperative. So, a researcher might set a 50 percent quota on respondents who identify themselves as white and leave the survey open to all other race/ethnicity choices.

Quantitative methods assign numbers and scores to the measurement of beliefs, attitudes, intentions, and behavior. To achieve such measurement, a researcher must first develop the specific and measurable constructs to be defined, collected, and measured. A construct can be thought of as building blocks or abstract concepts that can't really be observed. One example is "love." Love can be defined or measured in a million different ways from feelings to the ways in which people show affection. Still though, depending on the specific focus of the research aim, love can and should be broken down into specific and measurable quantifiable constructs.

Two important factors to keep in mind when conducting quantitative research using specific and measurable quantifiable constructs are *reliability* and *validity*. Reliability is the degree to which a measurement provides consistent data. Validity is the degree to which the researcher actually measures what they set out to measure. Therefore, quantitative research breaks down people's beliefs, attitudes, intentions, and behavior into specific and measurable constructs in an effort to gather reliable, consistent, and valid data with which to generalize an answer for the research aim.

Surveys, content analysis, and social network analysis can help answer strategic sport communicators' research questions and hypotheses through the collection of primary, quantitative data. With surveys, researchers ask respondents a series of specific questions and bound the possible answers by offering the respondent a choice of specific responses. In content analysis, content is surveyed to examine the presence or absence of certain material. Social network analysis reveals the interrelatedness, connectedness, and co-occurrences in the great vast world of strategic sport communication. The following sections explain each of these quantitative methods in detail.

Surveys

Surveys are another form of interviewing but within the confines of the participant selecting specific, defined answers. Instead of the open-ended questions asked in interviews or focus groups, respondents are instead asked a question and then offered a set of answers from which to choose. Surveys ask individuals about their beliefs, attitudes, intentions, and behaviors about the specific, measurable constructs regarding the research topic being investigated.

Close-ended questions offer a set of answer choices so that the researcher can assign numbers and scores to define, collect, and measure the operationalized construct that will aid the research aim. The answer choices for each question are either multiple choice, meaning there are options for the respondent to choose from, dichotomous (yes or no), or scaled, which is a measure of quantity: how much, how often, etc. (see Box 5.2).

BOX 5.2 Types of survey questions

Dichotomous: A respondent chooses between two options.

I **am/am not** a sports fan. (circle one)

Multiple Choice: A respondent chooses among three or more options.
   I consume sports by (select all that apply):

a)   Watching sports on television.
b)   Listening to sports on the radio
c)   Reading about sports in the newspaper.
d)   Attending sporting events.

   Scaled Responses: A respondent chooses how much or degree of intensity a respondent might engage in some belief, attitude, intention, or behavior along a scaled response. This is a five-point scale for a respondent who will select their personal level of likelihood regarding the following question:
   How likely are you to "trash talk" a rival fan after your team beat their team?
   Not at all likely (1) ... (2) ... (3) ... (4) ... (5) Very much likely

---

- Dichotomous: Choice is between two options.
- Multiple Choice: Choice is among three or more options.
- Scaled Responses: Designed to capture the intensity of a respondent's beliefs, attitudes, intentions, and behaviors.

Open-ended questions to which the respondent replies in his or her own words instead of selecting an offered set of answers, are sometimes included in quantitative surveys to gather complementary qualitative data. The responses can sometimes result in useful and informative data or the answers can be completely unusable. It is recommended that researchers keep open-ended questions to a minimum in quantitative surveys, especially those delivered online.

Data analysts call the survey question responses "variables" because responses vary from one respondent to another. Not everyone is the same amount of a sports fan, for example. Some people may be fair-weathered fans and some people may be die-hard fans, while still others may fall anywhere along that continuum. Every variable is either independent or dependent. An independent variable remains the same and is not manipulated when assessed or analyzed alongside another variable. Dependent variables are "dependent" upon how it is assessed or analyzed with other variables. For example, one might hypothesize that younger adults will rate higher than older adults on a fandom scale. In this scenario, the independent variable is age and the dependent variable is fandom.

The length and structure of the survey should be well thought-out before administering the survey. The length of the survey is a careful consideration because the researcher needs to balance the amount of information they wish to gather with the respondent burden it might require. In a general sense, surveys should be kept to a ten-minute completion time. Moreover, the delivery method of the survey is dependent upon your sample and the easiest way to reach your sample. Surveys can be delivered or conducted in person, on paper, through the mail, or online. Survey research companies can be paid to help reach a target sample, if the budget allows. It is always a best practice to pilot test your survey. Ask friends, family members or colleagues to take your survey before launching the survey to the intended sample. Piloting surveys before launch can help a researcher work out any kinks, such as whether any of the questions are too complicated, and can help save money from a wasted attempt. Piloting a survey also allows researchers to test data output and data analyses.

Software: SPSS, R or Excel for data analysis.

Content Analysis

Content analysis allows a researcher to collect data regarding the conceptual and relational conveyance of a topic within an artifact or set of artifacts. Artifacts can be news articles or segments, photos, movies, songs, and even sports replays—just to name a few examples. Social media is a rich source for content analysis, too. Social media sites are especially useful in conducting social network analysis using content analysis data, which will be discussed in the next section.

Content analysis is a surveying of content. The researcher "asks" specific questions regarding content within the particular artifact being researched. For example, a strategic communicator might want to research how the media covers a particular topic regarding sport in order to identify how a client might best contribute to that conversation. In other words, content analysis is a useful tool to keep a finger on the pulse of the social construction of sport. A researcher might ask: *What are people talking about? Why are they talking about that topic? Who is the focus? How are the stories being told, by whom, and how exactly are the storytellers framing each story? Is the sentiment of the coverage positive or negative?*

Content analysis also allows a researcher to ask specific questions. A researcher may need to examine the content within an artifact or set of artifacts for framing, themes, or sentiment regarding one specific sport entity of interest. Recall here that in public relations, reputation is considered a social construct made up of, "everything you do, everything you say, and everything everyone else says and thinks about you" (Hopwood et al., 2010, p. 17). Therefore, conducting a content analysis allows strategic communicators to gauge public opinion through public conversations in an effort to monitor a client's reputation. Questions a researcher might investigate when conducting content analysis research to assess a client's reputation include:

- How does media portray the league/team/athlete?
- How does media portray what the league/team/athlete does/says/how they operate?
- How does media portray what others have to say about the league/team/athlete?
- How are any of these matters discussed on social media sites by consumers?

The types of data that can be assessed in a content analysis include the presence, absence or prevalence of content and the sentiment with which the content is conveyed. There is manifest content, which is indisputably present content; and there is latent content, which is content presented with an underlying meaning. An example of manifest content is the date the news article was published. Sentiment is the tone of the message being conveyed. Sentiment should be surveyed as a dichotomous positive or negative by asking whether the article is mostly positive or mostly negative. Because sentiment can be so subjective, sentiment is considered a form of latent content.

News frames are often analyzed in content analyses because news frames help inform strategic sport communication campaigns. News frames can distinguish, for example, whether topics are being told in an episodic or thematic manner. Episodic news frames convey single occurrences, whereas thematic framing reports on the continuance of an issue (Iyengar, 1994). News frames can help to gauge the salience of an issue.

Co-occurrence is another important analysis that can be conducted using this quantitative method. The co-occurrence of entities in news reporting can help a researcher identify the social construction of a topic as well as whom the key individuals or entities are in regard to the topic. A co-occurrence content analysis involves the coders recording the manifest content of name of individual or companies, the frequencies of such mention, and whether any individual or companies are mentioned in the same paragraph. Recording these manifest occurrences can help enrich the analysis of the latent content by examining who is presented, the stance they represent, and how each co-occur throughout.

Similar to conducting a survey, a good sampling plan is first required to conduct a content analysis. A researcher will need to identify the artifact to code and the type of author or publisher of that artifact. The sample should be time bound in some sensible manner, too. If a researcher wants to examine how news organizations covered athlete health and safety regarding COVID-19, including any time-period prior to February 2019 would not yield effective results. Sampling for a content analysis is similar to sampling for a survey. Both a sampling frame and a sampling technique are necessary components of this research method.

Once a researcher identifies and selects the sample, a codebook and codesheet are created. A codebook is a detailed document outlining how exactly a coder is to review each artifact and survey that artifact for the specific data to be collected. Full and thorough instructions are imperative here so that any person, no matter their level of knowledge on the topic, could become a coder and coding would be consistent among coders at a percent beyond just chance. This is called intercoder reliability. Intercoder reliability should be tested using a small percentage of the sample before the full coding process is conducted. Intercoder reliability, like pilot testing a survey, helps to work out any discrepancies among each variable being captured for analysis. Intercoder reliability is achieved when at least 70 percent agreement or greater is achieved across coders per variable. Once intercoder reliability is reached, the rest of the coding may begin.

Once this primary data set is collected, data analysis can help answer the research questions or hypotheses to aid in the research aim. For example, variable frequencies can be reported and inferential statistics run. Using the example of a researcher investigating how news organizations covered athlete health and safety regarding COVID-19, variable frequencies can report how many athletes the news organization reported on and how many of those were report as testing positive or testing negative. Inferential statistics could involve a statistical analysis using crosstabs regarding the article that reported positive test results and article sentiment (i.e., positive or negative). One might hypothesize that news coverage will be more negative in sentiment when reporting on an athlete testing positive for COVID-19 than when an athlete tests negative for COVID-19.

Pro tip: Dr. Deen Freelon, an associate professor of media studies at the University of North Carolina at Chapel Hill, created a website and program to aid researchers in calculating intercoder reliability. The complex statistical program is called ReCal. ReCal can be accessed at dfreelon.com. *If you use this program, please cite the website and ReCal program in your data reporting section.

Software to aid with content analysis: SPSS, R or Excel for quantitative data analysis; MAXQDA for qualitative data analysis; ProQuest and NVivo for data collection.

Social Network Analysis

Strategic sport communication is rooted in relationships because relationships are the root of communication. Humans communicate with the people they know or the people they can reach. We often hear the term "communication networks" or we call social media "networks" or "networking sites." This is because networks are the encampments of relationships where communication can flow.

Social network analysis, as a research method, is not a social networking site like Twitter, Snapchat, or Instagram, but instead an investigation into an individual's or organization's network of people or organizations with whom they are connected in some operationalized way. Therefore, a social network is a person's or entity's online and offline connections. Those connections can be operationalized as descriptive, relational, or explanatory ties. A descriptive tie between people can be sex or race, for example. So, someone might ask you to name all the women you know. A relational connection can be categorized as friends or family members. For example, you might be asked to list all the women you know and with whom you are related. You might list a mother, sister, aunt, or grandmother to whom you have such relational ties. An explanatory connection can be any specific and measureable construct that is the aim of your research. So, an explanatory tie can be love or an explanatory tie can be someone you believe to be a sports fan. In this scenario, you might be asked to list any women you know with whom you are related and who you believe to be sports fans. Your responses would make up this specific social network that is unique to you, the women you know and are related to, and are sports fans. In this egocentric network we just created, you are the ego. An ego in a social network is the central node to which all other nodes are connected. An ego network, like the one we just constructed with your descriptive, relational, and explanatory connections (i.e., women who are related to you and are sports fans), depicts the relationships you have with women sports fans. Each person we ask this set of questions to would report a network that would differ or vary from the one we just created. Whole networks are another type of social network analysis structure to research, which is discussed next.

Social networks can range from ego networks—the social network of one—to whole networks, which is a social network that includes all possible connected relationships for a specific, operationalized network. A whole network, for example, could be a workplace. Perhaps a sport franchise like the Ultimate Fighting Championship (UFC). According to Wikipedia, UFC is "an American mixed martial arts promotion company based in Las Vegas, Nevada, which is owned and operated by Endeavor Group Holdings along with Silver Lake Partners, Kohlberg Kravis Roberts, and MSD Capital via Zuffa, LLC." Every individual who works for UFC and its owners and operators could be defined as a specific and measureable whole social network. The ties between all employees can be relational (i.e., they work together as UFC employees) or they can be descriptive (i.e., the owners or the athletes/fighters) or explanatory (those who make more than $250K/year). No matter how we define this whole network, the individuals, or nodes, are interconnected in some manner and those connections are called ties.

Social networks are therefore made up of nodes and ties. These nodes and ties can be operationalized in virtually any manner. The nodes in the ego network above are you and the individuals (nodes) you listed (ties). The more detailed the questions became, the more specific the operationalization of the nodes (you and the women you know, to whom you are related, who are sports fans). The ties between the nodes are operationalized here as familial ties. The ties in the whole network were operationalized as people who work together under the UFC organizational umbrella.

Social network analysis relates to transmedia campaign strategies in countless ways. Knowing who or what is interconnected and exactly how those connections are formed or strengthened can make or break a strategic sport communication campaign. Communication is often operationalized as a tie between nodes in social networks. Communication among people is often observed and measured using social network analysis. Communication among people on social networking sites is also often observed and measured using social network analysis.

When creating a social network as a primary data collection method, it is imperative to first operationalize the nodes and the specific ties of interest; and the simpler, the better. A researcher might wish to collect every NFL team's corporate partners (see Figure 5.1). The nodes will be the 32 NFL teams and each team's respective corporate partners. The ties between the teams and the corporate partners represent the business partnership between the two. This network then can be enhanced by adding strength to the tie between teams and corporate partners. The length of time a team and a corporation have been partnered, or the amount of money exchanged annually, are both possible indicators to depict the strength of the tie between these entities.

Social network analysis can be paired with other primary data collection methods, too. For example, social network analysis can build upon content analysis data by conducting a co-occurrence analysis. A co-occurrence analysis identifies who or what co-occurs with one another. As an example of this approach, a researcher might want to examine how often Roger Goodell and Colin Kaepernick are both mentioned in news articles that discuss social justice issues in sport. Social network analysis can also be conducted using survey data. A researcher can ask respondents with whom they have discussed the #TakeAKnee movement, who those people are relationally to the respondent, and how much they perceive each of those people to be sports fans.

Once you have operationalized the social network that will help answer the research questions and hypotheses at hand, or help to come to some conclusion regarding your specific research aim, data analysis should be conducted. Network centrality measurements are the most common data analysis measurements related to social network analysis. This is because social network theories explain that those nodes most central within a network will have the most ties to other nodes in the network, and having the most ties offers the best access to resources. Think back to either the ego network or the whole network created above. If you needed an extra ticket to an upcoming sporting event, the larger your network and the most central you are within that network, the better your chances that someone around you may have an extra ticket or know where to get you that extra ticket.

A UFC fighter in the whole network is going to be central within the whole UFC network. The fighter will know management, communicators, and trainers, and will likely encounter various other staff members. The fighter will thus have a high degree centrality. Degree centrality is the number of connections or ties a node has to other nodes within the network. Eigenvector centrality represents the number of connections a node's connections enjoy. So, the UFC fighter is connected to managers, communicators, trainers, and other general staff members. The managers are likely to have connections with almost everybody inside this whole network and additional business-related connections outside the UFC network—namely those organizations that are co-owners of UFC. That manager's connections thus strengthen the fighter's reach throughout the whole network and provide the best access to the richest resources.

Centrality measurements help a researcher tell a story. Probably one of the best aspects of social network analysis is the ability to depict the network through visual aids. A sociogram is a visual aid to help convey the story regarding the social network. FIgure 5.1 showcases the nodes (NFL teams and their corporate partners), ties (the business connection among the teams and corporate partners), and centrality positions (e.g., degree centrality) of this specific network. This network sociogram shows that Anheuser-Busch is the most central node amongst all team and corporate partnerships. This is because Anheuser-Busch is partnered with all but four NFL teams, so this node's number of connections are the highest among all nodes in the network. The story we can tell here? Beer is the centerpiece of American football. #BudBowl

Software: NodeXL Pro or NVivo.

Deliverables

Every research project should include:

- a list of research questions and hypotheses;
- a sampling plan that includes a sampling strategy and a sampling technique;
- a list of specific and measurable constructs that are operationalized well enough to be reliable, consistent, and valid constructs;
- a table, chart, infographic, or sociogram as a visual aid;
- data analysis, results, and how those results answer the research questions and hypotheses.

  Survey: RQs/Hs, Sampling Plan, Electronic Survey Questionnaire, Survey Results, Data Analysis, a Table, and a list of answers for the RQs/Hs.

  Content Analysis: RQs/Hs, Sampling Plan, Codebook and Codesheet, Intercoder Reliability, Data Analysis, Data Results, a visual aid, and a list of answers for the RQs/Hs.

  Social Network Analysis: RQs/Hs, Sampling Plan, Data Analysis, Data Results, a Sociogram, and a list of answers for the RQs/Hs.

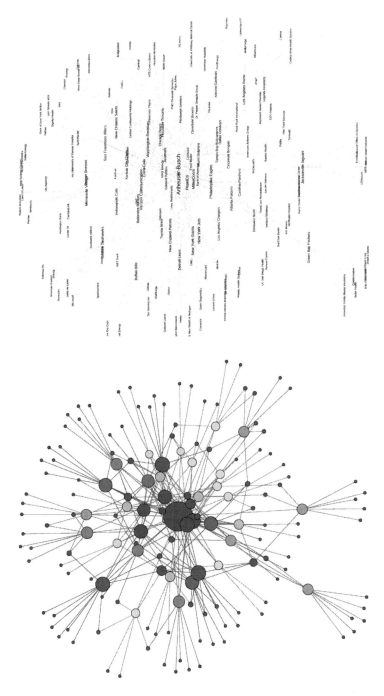

Figure 5.1 Sociograms. Pictured are two sociograms of the NFL teams and each team's corporate partners—one without node labels and one with node labels.

Running Example: Opportunity for Watford FC

The scanning revealed the potential opportunity of developing a sensory room to serve fans on the autism spectrum and their families. Research is used to understand whether or not this is a viable opportunity. Watford could begin with secondary research by reviewing the data on what percentage of the population of the UK are ASD. That data reveals that in the UK, about 1.1 percent of the population is on the autism spectrum. That percentage suggests there is a need for a sensory room. Watford could contact the local autism charity to get information about the percentage of the population locally that are on the autism spectrum. But the need can be examined further through primary research by investigating the Watford fans more closely.

Watford could conduct a survey of fans to identify roughly what percentage of their fans have a family member on the autism spectrum and how likely they are to use a sensory room. If the results indicated very few fans have family members on the autism spectrum or were unlike to use the room, the opportunity is not very good. However, Watford has already received requests from two families about a sensory room. We will assume the survey data were supportive of people wanting to have and to use sensory room meaning there is a true opportunity. Watford could conduct interviews with fans who have family members on the autism spectrum. The interviews could begin with the two families that had already contacted Watford about sensory rooms. The interviews would provide greater insights into the possible use of the room and the value the fans attached to a sensory room.

A final piece of research would involve costs. Watford needs to get an estimate for how much the sensory room will cost to build and to staff. This research would include how much of the cost would be covered by the Premier League fund for sensory rooms and the charities willing to provide money for the construction. Such information allows Watford to determine the final cost of the room for the club and if that cost fits within the team's budget. An opportunity can be impractical if it is too costly. The data suggests there is both a need among Watford fans and the cost is minimal and within budget. Based upon the data from the research Watford decides to pursue the opportunity by building the sensory room.

Running Example: Threat for the Los Angeles Dodgers

The need to address racism following the spring 2020 protests in the U.S. could be a threat for the Los Angeles Dodgers. That threat comes from the felt need to speak out against racism. The Los Angeles Dodgers could begin by reviewing the many public opinion polls (secondary data) that ask people whether or not they expect organizations to speak about racism. A good example of the secondary data is Edelman's report "Brands and Racial Justice in America." In the Edelman study, the secondary data indicates 60 percent of the American people are willing to buy or boycott based upon how the brand responds to protests for social justice while 56 percent feel brands have a moral obligation to take a stand on social justice (Edelman, 2020). The Dodgers also should look for studies conducted specifically in the Los Angeles area to see if their community is more or less committed than what the national data suggests. Generally, the secondary data is supporting that the threat is real and salient.

The Dodgers could conduct primary research to get a feel for how the social justice issue is resonating among its fan base. One option would be a content analysis of fan comments on various Dodger social media platforms and fan sites. The Dodgers could conduct a qualitative analysis of the comments for themes (thematic analysis). If a need to address social justice is a theme, it supports the importance of a threat. The Dodgers also could conduct a formal content analysis of the comments to determine what percent of the fans are expressing support of social justice concerns. We can assume a large percentage of the fan comments were supportive of social justice reinforcing the need to address racism and social justice as a threat. Remember, threats and opportunities are connected to one another. Acting on a threat is an opportunity if it is handled properly. Based upon the data for the research, the Dodgers decide there is a need to make a statement and to take some action about racism.

References

Edelman (2020). Brands and racial justice in America. Available online at https://www.edelman.com/sites/g/files/aatuss191/files/2020-06/2020%20 Edelman%20Trust%20Barometer%20Specl%20Rept%20Brands%20and%20 Racial%20Justice%20in%20America.pdf.

Hopwood, M., Kitchin, P., & Skinner, J. (2010). *Sport public relations and communication*. Burlington, MA: Butterworth-Heinemann.

Iyengar, S. (1994). *Is anyone responsible? How television frames political issues*. Chicago: University of Chicago Press.

6 Planning
Creating Guidance for Action

In general, planning provides guidance and helps things run more smoothly. Let's say you are taking a trip to Disney World. Planning can be the difference between a great trip and a misadventure. A great trip is one where you get to ride the attractions you want and not spend more time waiting in lines than enjoying the vacation. Your planning would include when to go. Ideally you pick a time when park attendance is lower and not high-volume days such as around Christmas or during spring breaks. Lower attendance means a general reduction in wait times. Disney World offers fast passes that allow you pick a time to ride an attraction (a one-hour window) and to have quick access to the attraction. You can book fast passes 90 days before you arrive. Early booking of fast passes helps to ensure you get access to the attractions you want with a short amount of wait time. You can check current wait times on the My Disney app to find attractions with the shortest wait times. Finally, you can reserve dining months in advance to reduce the wait time for eating. These are but four examples of how planning for your Disney World vacation can reduce the wait time and increase the enjoyment.

For strategic communication, planning not only helps you to save time but can save money by preventing mistakes and wasted effort. We can think of most strategic communication efforts as projects. Projects are temporary (have a specific start and end date), and create a unique result, product, or service. Projects are common in organizations but poor planning can be costly with projects. In the U.S., for instance, 10 percent of a project's budget is wasted on poor execution (PMI, 2014). The use of planning tools, such as a project schedule, has been found to increase project success (Patanakul, Iewwaongchoroern, & Milosevic, 2010). Project management is the discipline dedicate to improving projects. Project management is defined as "applying tools, techniques, skills and knowledge to project activities to bring about successful results and meet the project requirements" (Heldman, 2009, p. 7). Planning is a key element of project management. In this chapter we are applying principles from strategic communication and project management to explain the key elements of planning in strategic communication efforts. Planning begins with an understanding of goals and objectives. Planning requires a command of the essential elements of strategic communication including target segments, core messages, and media. Finally, it

DOI: 10.4324/9781003031161-7

is important to understand the basics of how to use these materials in the creation of basic planning documents.

Basic Terms: Goals and Objectives

Strategy is a guide for action and the idea of strategic communication demands that communication be purposeful. Goals and objectives are critical to giving purpose to your communication efforts. In this section we define goals and objectives as the anchors for strategic communication. A goal is "a general statement of what you hope to achieve" with a communication effort (Coombs, 2005, p. 364). Goals are the general direction you want to go with a communication effort including what you generally hope to achieve with the communication. Goals are a starting point for developing strategy that must be refined into objectives to create more precise guidance for a communication effort. Objectives serve to establish what is expected from your strategic communication effort. Consider the following example. You start with a goal of raising money for charity. That is a general idea that you will raise money and it will go to charity. But there is a lack of detail about how you will do this. An objective might be "To raise $15,000 for the local Boys and Girls Club." Now you know how much you intend to raise and who will receive the money. The increased specificity makes it easier to begin planning how you will raise the money. Along the way, objectives help to establish your criteria for success—how you will judge the success of failure of your communication effort. In our example, the criteria for success is raising the $15,000.

There are actually three types of objectives: output, outreach, and outcome. Each type of objective can contribute value to the strategic communication effort. Output objectives are the actions you take in developing and executing the communication effort. Think of output objectives as the tasks needed to complete the communication effort. We will talk more about specific outputs in the discussion of the planning documents later in this chapter. Outreach objectives are the actions of intermediaries that contribute to your communication effort. Frequently a communication effort will include having the news media, bloggers, or influencers relaying your message to your target audience. For instance, the news media might carry a story about your fundraising effort or a blogger might write a post about it. The key is some intermediary is needed to pass your message along to people who consume messages created by the intermediary. These intermediaries are known as gatekeepers. A gatekeeper controls access in some way. Bloggers, for example, decide the content of their own blog posts while editors control what content appears in print and digital publications.

Outcome objectives are the change you hope to produce in the target audience (Laskin, 2016). The change needs to be specific and measurable. This might include a specific amount you hope to achieve or a percent increase or decrease in an amount. Let's return to the fund raising example. The objective we provided was a specific amount, $15,000. Or you might present the outcome objectives as a percentage increase in donations over the previous year's fundraiser such as "Increase the amount of money raised for the Boys and Girls Club by 17 percent." Outcome objectives help to establish the criteria for success. You can count the money to determine if you raised $15,000 or compare the results from this year's fundraiser to the previous year to determine if there was at least a 17 percent increase.

Outcome objectives seek to produce change. Ideally, we want the target audience to do something as a result of their experiencing the communication effort. In our running example, we want people to donate money for charity. When the communication effort leads to behavior change, that is called moving the needle. However, there are two other types of changes a communication effort might create: knowledge and attitude. Knowledge seeks to create awareness and to have people learn new information. People will now know something after engaging with your message that they did not know before. Attitudes are how people feel about something such as an organization, a product, or a service. Communication efforts seek to cultivate favorable attitudes toward an organization, its products, and/or its services. We can think of knowledge, attitude, and behavior as building upon one another. Again, we can use the donation for charity objective. People need to know about a charity effort (knowledge) and think positively about it (attitude) before donating money (behavior). Knowledge and attitude can contribute to influencing behavior. You communicate about the fundraiser to people so they know it exits, will think donating is a good idea, and will then donate. The objectives for your strategic communication effort can be a mix of knowledge, attitude, and/or behavior.

While we have been talking about the goals and objectives of your strategic communication effort, you must never lose sight of the larger organizational goals. Whether a team or an individual, there are two larger goals in sport: generate revenue and social approval. Revenue is what keeps a team or an athlete competing. Consider the problems during COVID-19 for sports teams when gate revenues and broadcast rights began to disappear. Strategic sport communication efforts should support revenue generation in some way. It is not always easy to prove how the strategic communication effort contributes to revenue but the link to revenue should be considered in the planning process.

Social approval is "an overarching construct to describe the more intuitive and affective perceptions inherent in the social evaluation of an organization" (Bundy & Pfarrer, 2015, p. 348). Generally, social approval is whether or not people like an organization. A favorable collective perception is called a social approval asset because it can benefit the organization in many ways including helping to generate revenue. An unfavorable collective perception is a social disapproval liability (Pfarrer et al., 2010). Reputation is a common form of social approval. There is a long history of linking strategic communication to reputation building (e.g., Foreman & Argenti, 2005). Hence, it is relatively easy to link a strategic sport communication effort with enhancing social approval. Social approval is valuable in part because it can intensify identification. As noted earlier, social identification helps to explain fan behavior including spending money. The more strongly a fan identifies with a team or player, the more likely that fan is to watch and to spend money on the sport (Hickman, 2015).

In our fund-raising example, supporting a charity that your target audience likes should result in your target audience linking your organization more—enhancing social approval. The ability to enhance social approval has an indirect effect on your revenue because the more strongly people identify with your organization, the more likely they are to attend an event or buy merchandise. A communication effort to promote new partial season ticket packages, on the other hand, has a direct effect on revenue because you can track the effect of the communication effort on the sales of the new packages. You could provide a link from the Instagram messages to ticket sales. Your claim of increases sales becomes stronger when people are using the links to buy partial season tickets. The link helps you to identify those partial season ticket sales that are directly connected to the Instagram message in your strategic communication effort. The important lesson is that your communication objectives should be linked to the larger organizational goals of revenue and social approval. In addition to these two larger goals, organizations can have specific business objectives. This means you should be thinking about how your strategic communication objectives fit with specific business objectives as well. The most effective strategic communication efforts support organizational goals and objectives rather than simply pursuing just the communication objectives.

Target Segments

The target audience are the people you intend your message to reach and to affect in some way. Various terms are used instead of target audience including publics, stakeholders, and constituents. The name does not really matter. What does matter is that you know the nature of your target audience and why you are targeting them. The term target audience is overly broad. The nature of your target audience is a matter of segmentation. You are looking for ways to divide up the people you hope to reach into useful segments. Through segmentation, you are trying to understand what factors people share in your target audience because you cannot craft a message unless you know who you are trying to appeal to with that message. It is the shared characteristics of the target audience that provide insights into what should appeal to specific subgroups of your target audience. You then craft a message that embodies the values and ideas that should appeal to a specific segment. The assumption is that the shared characteristics help to predict what is appealing to the segment and how they might react to your message. It is more precise to talk about target segments than a target audience.

There are various ways to create groups for your target segments including demographics and psychographics. Demographics are common ways to segment audience and include age, gender, ethnicity, income, occupation, religion, and education level. Again, the belief is that people who share demographic factors will react in a similar manner to messages. You can even combine various demographic factors when creating a profile of your target audience. Demographics are useful if it makes sense to segment your target audience in this way. Age, for example, is a useful demographic when selecting your media mix. As we will discuss further in the next section, social media platforms have different age profiles for users. Think about what demographic factors can help you gain some insights into your target segments. If you were seeking to target parents of school age children, your demographic is likely to be an age range of 26 to 34 years old.

Just using demographics is limiting but you can add greater insights by using psychographics. Understanding people's interests and values falls under the general heading of psychographics. Common psychographics include lifestyles, activities, and interests. Understanding how people live their lives, what they do in their spare time, and what hobbies they pursue gives you insight into their values—what they find to be important. The psychographics can give you ideas about what themes to include in your message. Consider the example of holding a 5K race to raise money for charity. What psychographic factors could be related to participating in a 5K charity race? Avid runners, people looking to create a healthy lifestyle, and those who volunteer or donate to charities are possible psychographics to consider. The first two groups would be interested in the fitness aspect of the 5K while the third group would find the altruism aspect of the event appealing. Psychographics provide insights into the values of your target segments. Combining demographics and psychographics provide critical information for developing themes for your message and media selection, the next two points we will cover.

Core Messages

The core message is the central theme in your message. The core message is the foundation for your message and is sometimes called the key idea (Vos, Otte, & Linders, 2003). The theme should embody the values that should be appealing to your target audience. You should think about how each core message might appeal to each of your specific target segments. We can return to the 5K run used to raise money for charity to illustrate the connection. One core message might be fitness to appeal to the runners and people concerned about fitness. A second core message might be ways the 5K can benefit the local charity to appeal to those interested in altruism. The core message is just a starting point. You will then decide how to translate the core messages into the specific messages you create for the strategic communication effort. The next chapter explores the various factors to consider when translating the core messages into specific messages.

Media Selection

Media refers to the communication channels used to transmit a message to a target segment. In other words, media captures the various ways you have for delivering a message to your target segment. Typically, you have a mix of media you would use in a strategic communication effort. The media you select must be the media consumed by your target segments. If your media are not a match to your target segments, the people you desire to affect will never even be exposed to your message. Improper media selection will doom a strategic communication effort. We placed the discussion of target segments before media because you cannot select the media until you know who you are trying to reach with the message. It is imperative that you know what media your target segments consume. Each medium (the singular form of media) has a unique demographic and psychographic profile for its users. Do not get blinded by the number of users of a particular medium. Social media platforms like to brag about how many users they have. If a particular social media platform has 1 billion users but has weak coverage of your target segments, it really holds little value for you. Do research to see if the media match the demographics and/or psychographics of your target segments. Demographic information is easy to find for various media. Psychographics might take more effort to uncover but logic can help the process. Look at the content of the specific medium or social media account to see if it fits the interests of your target segments. We can compare Instagram and Twitter on some basic demographics. Twitter users are predominantly male while Instagram is more female than male. We find 75 percent of Instagram users are aged 18 to 24 while only 44 percent of Twitter users fit that age group (Barnhart, 2021). The Facebook page of a local running club might be an idea medium for the 5K fund raiser. The people belonging to the page are interested in running and live locally meaning they not only have motivation but access to your 5K event.

There are four categories of media: earned, owned, shared, and paid. You will select various options from these four categories for your strategic communication effort. Figure 6.1 is a visual depiction of what is known as the PESO model. The PESO model was developed by strategic communication professional Gini Dietrich at Spin Sucks. Earned media reflect the basic idea of publicity—a public relations message prompts a source to create a story favorable about the organization. Public relations was built on publicity through media relations. Professionals would send out news releases or pitch story ideas to people in the news media. Publicity is created when a member of the news media uses the information from the professional to create a favorable news story. An example would be an organization was about to launch a new product. News releases were sent to various news media outlets about the qualities and benefits of the new product. If the news outlets then ran a story about the new products and its positive qualities, publicity had been created. The earned category reflects the digital dimension of public relations. Professionals today engage in blogger and influencer relations in

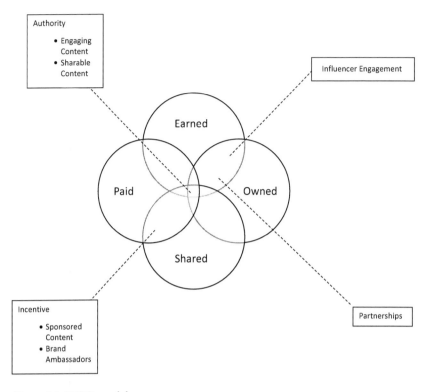

Figure 6.1 PESO model.
Source: Dietrich (2020).

addition to the more traditional media relations. Regardless of the target, earned media is based on trying to influence what some valued gatekeeper writes about your organization, product, or service.

Valued gatekeepers are any entity that create messages consumed by your target segment. News writers, editors, influencers, podcasters, and bloggers are all gatekeepers. For earned media, gatekeepers decide what stories are used by a news outlet, what information in posted by an influencer, or what topic is used in a blog post. For the strategic communication professional, there is a lack of control with earned media. You do not know if a gatekeeper will use your message or how the gatekeeper might use the message. We have qualified effective publicity as the stimulation of positive messages. If could be that your effort to generate a story creates a negative reaction from the gatekeepers and they write an unfavorable story. You cannot control how the gatekeeper might use the information you have sent to them. This means there is an element of risk to earned media. One way to minimize the risk is to understand the gatekeepers. What do they typically write or talk about? Only send information that fits with the topics the gatekeepers typically address. Gatekeepers dislike being sent information they would never use because the messages are a waste of their time. Understanding gatekeepers reduces the likelihood of a negative reaction and increases the likelihood they might use your information. If a podcaster only talks about college sports, do not pitch them an idea about a professional team.

Owned media are controlled by the strategic communication professional because these are the messages created in-house by the organization. Web sites, brochures, newsletters, and other digital documents are common examples of owned media. If you control the content and distribution of the message, it is owned. Leagues have been developing their own broadcast networks in both professional and college sports. The Big 10 Network was a pioneer in college sports while all the major sports leagues in the U.S. have their own networks such as MLB Network and the NFL Network. Even some professional teams have their own networks such as Manchester United (MUTV) and the Toronto Maple Leafs (Leafs TV). Any channel where the strategic communication professional has the power to create and to distribute the content is owned media.

Shared is the "new" category driven by the digital environment. Shared media is the use of social media channels by the strategic communication professionals. Tweets, Facebook posts, TikTok videos, Pinterest images, and YouTube videos are all shared media along with any other social media platform that currently exists or will exist in the future. Immediately, your shared media reach those who follow or somehow encounter your social media accounts. Hashtags are used to make your content easier to find and to track. An added benefit is the ability of people to pass along your information by sharing it with others. A perfect example of that would be a retweet. Sharing extends the reach of a message beyond your followers to include the followers of those sharing your message. Sharing of a message is one of the critical social media metrics an organization should monitor. See Box 6.1 for list of common social media metrics. Social media metrics are essential for evaluation, too. Shared media have the advantage of being relatively low cost and creating the ability to engage directly with your target segment.

BOX 6.1 Social media metrics

Potential Reach: number of people who could see a post
   Total Number of Mentions x Followers of Accounts that Mention You = Potential Reach
   Social Share of Voice: your mentions compares to competitor mentions
   Brand Mentions + Competition Mentions/Total Mentions x 100 = Social Share of Voice
   Post Reach: how many people have seen a post
   Reach/Total Number of Followers x 100 = Post Reach
   Amplification rate: ration of shares per post to total followers

Number of shares/Number of followers x 100 = Amplification Rate

Applause rate: number of approvals (likes & favorites) relative to total followers

Total Approval Actions/Total Followers x 100 = Applause Rate

Virality rate: number of people sharing a post relative to number of unique views

Number of Shares/Number of Impressions x 100 = Virality Rate

Average Engagement rate: number of reactions a post receives relative to total followers

Total Likes, Comments & Shares/Total Followers x 100 = Average Engagement Rate

Conversation rate: the ration of comments per post to the number of followers

Total Comments/Total Followers x 100= Conversation rate

Conversion rate: number of visitors who take action on a page after clicking in a post compared to total visitors

Conversions/Total Clicks x 100 = Conversion Rate

Click-through rate: how often people click on an action link in a post

Total Clicks/Total Impressions x 100 = Click-through Rate

Social media conversion rate: total number of conversions coming from social media

Social Media Conversions/Total Conversions x 100 = Social Media Conversion Rate (Chen, 2020)

Paid is when the strategic communicator pays money to have a message placed on a channel. Paid offers control over the placement and content of a message but has a higher price tag than the other three media categories. Traditionally, advertising has been the primary example of paid media. However, sponsored content is important now. Sponsored content is when you pay to have a publisher create and distribute your messages. You can sponsor articles, videos, infographics, Tweets, Snapchat Stories, YouTube videos, Pins, Podcast episodes, and any other form of social media content you can list. If you use a social media account, odds are you have experienced sponsored content. Sponsored content is marked so that a user knows when someone has paid to put that message in front of them. Sports marketing is another form of paid channel. Sometimes the sport itself is used to market a product or service. Naming rights to a stadium, digital signage of official sponsors in stadiums, and jersey sponsorships are highly visible forms of sports marketing. That Nike swoosh on your favorite team's jersey did not get there by accident or for free.

There is no one, perfect medium for reaching any target segment. That is why in strategic communication we talk about a media mix. Table 6.1 provides a quick summary of the advantages and disadvantages of the four media categories. There are four evaluative factors: (1) cost, (2) control,

Table 6.1 Advantages and disadvantages of media options

MEDIA	Evaluative Factors			
	Cost	Control	Endorsement	Engagement Potential
Earned	Low	Weak	Strong	Mixed potential
Owned	Low	Strong	Weak	Limited potential
Shared	Low	Strong	Mixed	Strong potential
Paid	High	Strong	Weak	Limited potential

(3) endorsement, and (4) engagement potential. Cost is the expense of the medium. Paid is by far the most expensive medium. The other three are low cost because the work is done as part of people's regular strategic communication jobs. The cost is low but can rise the more time a person or persons need to commit to the medium. Control refers to the ability of the strategic communication professional to determine the content and timing of delivery of a message in a particular channel. Earned media have very low control. Endorsement the degree to which a message indicates a third-party endorsement of the message—some entity outside of the organization supports the message. Earned has the strongest endorsement and when others re-post your shared content there is an element of endorsement. Engagement potential refers to the ability of stakeholders to like, comment, and share the message. Shared media has the strongest engagement potential. Earned is mixed because influencers sharing a message has high engagement potential while traditional media sharing a message has much lower engagement potential.

You need to decide what combination of media might be most useful for your strategic communication effort. It is common for strategic communication teams to begin by brainstorming possible ways to reach the target segments. You then need to assess the ideas you have created in the brainstorm. Your assessment should be based on the ability of the media to reach the target segment, the fit between your messages and the media, and your budget. As noted earlier, media that do not reach your target segment have no value. Your first assessment should be to check that the fit with the target segment is accurate. You have a core message. Does that message fit with the media? Consider if there are specific visual or text elements you plan to use and if the media can accommodate those considerations. If your message will center on a text message with limited graphics, does Twitter or TikTok make more sense and why? You may need to refine your media selection as you develop your messages more completely in the next step of the strategic communication process. Finally, budget is a reality because you cannot spend money you do not have. If you cannot afford a medium, you should not include it in your final media mix. The next section on planning documents returns to the importance of budgets in the strategic communication process.

Figure 6.2 Scope triangle.

Planning Documents

Projects require planning and planning is more efficient when there are planning documents to guide people. Your planning documents include the project schedule, the budget, and the risk management plan. In this section we will focus on the project schedule which details what tasks need to be completed and the timeline for their completion. Every project is driven by time, quality, and cost. The project must be done on time, be of sufficient quality, and be within the budget. Together, the three factors form the Scope Triangle illustrated in Figure 6.2. The three factors are related and changing one can affected the others. For instance, if you have a set time for a project to be completed, the quality of the project will be a function of the budget. You only have so much time to complete the project and the quality you can produce within that timeframe is a direct reflection of the money you have to spend. That means more money is equal to greater quality when you have a set period of time to complete the project. Similarly, if time is reduced but you want the same level of quality for the project, you will need additional money to accomplish that goal. Just remember that changes in time, quality, or costs changes how you approach and complete the project.

The project schedule allows you to plan out the work that needs to be done to complete the strategic communication effort. Gannt charts are a common way to visualize a project schedule. In a Gannt chart, the tasks are listed down the left side of the page and the time for completing the tasks are list across the top of the page. See Box 6.2 for more information about a Gannt chart. Software programs such as Microsoft Project can be used to create you planning documents. As the description to the Gannt chart suggests, the project schedule is all about time and tasks. It tells you what needs to be done and when it needs to be done. You can even go further and include who is assigned to each task and the cost of each task. The project schedule lets you know if your project is progressing on time, falling behind, or is ahead of schedule.

BOX 6.2 Gantt charts

A Gantt chart is a visual representation of a project that plots tasks over time using a version of a bar chart. A typical Gantt has tasks or activities listed in the left side of the chart, while time runs across the top of the chart. The chart is named for engineer Henry Gantt who popularized its use; however, the Polish engineer Karol Adamiecki used a version prior to Gantt's work. You can even show relationships between tasks and highlight milestones with a Gantt chart. Microsoft's Project Management software has a Gantt chart view. People working on the project can easily share the digital version and update the chart as tasks are completed. The Gantt chart provides a simple, visual check on the project's progress.

To create a project schedule, you begin with what is called the work breakdown structure (WBS). In the WBS, you begin to break the project into smaller pieces until you feel you have all the major tasks identified. The tasks include what you need to do to create the strategic communication effort such as create social media posts and the work needed to manage the project such as meetings and risk management efforts (Dionisio, 2019). Once you have the major tasks, you can enter them into Microsoft Project using the Gantt chart view. You need to name each major task so it is easy for those reading the project schedule to understand what needs to be done. Once the major tasks are entered you will subdivide them into sub-tasks. The sub-tasks are the steps you need to take to complete the major task. The project schedule should identify milestones. Milestones are significant events in the project such as the completion of key deliverables. A deliverable is a "product or capacity necessary to complete a project" (Dionisio, 2019, p. 35). Examples of deliverables include budgets, images to be used in Instagram posts, and text for Facebook posts.

The next step is to determine how the various tasks relate to one another. In a project, you cannot start all the major tasks at once because of what is knowns as dependencies. Dependencies are the "timing relationships between tasks" that require you to sequence tasks in a particular order. There are three types of dependencies you might have in a project. Mandatory dependency is the most basic type and is when one task starting depends on the completion of another task. For example, you cannot announce the location of an event until you secure the venue for the event. Resource dependency is when a resource cannot be used simultaneously. People on your team are resources. If a person is doing multiple tasks, that person must work on one task at a time. Neither a person nor piece of equipment can be in two places at once. An external dependency is when you need an external actor or resource to complete for a task. The task cannot begin until the outside action or resource arrives (Dionisio, 2019). You might hire an outside vendor to compete a task or to supply a resource that affects your ability to complete other tasks. If an outside vendor is supplying tables and chairs for your event, for instance, you cannot begin placing items for a silent auction on those tables until the vendor sets up the tables or you must be sure your porta-potties arrive for your 5K race before you have people begin to assemble for the race.

The challenge for the team is to identify the various dependencies among the tasks. The task that comes first is called the predecessor while the task that follows is called the successor. There can be four variations of dependencies. A finish-to-start dependency means the predecessor must be completed before you can start the successor task. A start-to-start dependency in when the two tasks must start at the same time. The finish-to-finish dependency is when both tasks must be completed at the same time. The start-to-finish dependency is when the predecessor can be completed only once the successor has started (Dionisio, 2019). Once you have identified the dependencies, you can enter those into Microsoft Project so that the project schedule includes a visual display of the dependencies. Once you have the tasks assigned you are half of the way through your schedule. The other half is estimating time.

According to project management experts, "the most challenging aspects of managing a project is estimating how long a task will take to complete" (Dionisio, 2019, p. 65). Experience is your best resource when estimating the time of a task. The more experience you have with a task, the easier it is to estimate the time for that task. Remember, time is one of the major factors in a project and each project has a delivery date that must be met—the deadline. The project must be done by the deadline! Missing a deadline is unacceptable in strategic communication. To estimate the time to complete a task, the following formula is often used: Time expected = (Optimistic + 4 x Realistic + Pessimistic)/6. Let's use a basic task such as upper-management approval of a message. From experience you know approval takes about five days but has been completed as quickly as two days but could take up to 14 days if certain people are out of the office. Your calculation would be 2 + 4(5) + 14/6 = 6 days. Optimistic is the shortest amount of time and is the situation when everything goes perfectly. Realistic time is more conservative because you anticipate there will be some delays. Pessimistic is the worst-case scenario where everything goes wrong. Once you have assigned time to each task, you enter that into your schedule. Now you will know how long the project will take by examining the time for each task and the dependencies between the tasks. You need to make sure the time to complete the strategic communication project fits the deadline for a project. If a strategic communication project will take eight weeks but the deadline is in six weeks, you need to rethink the strategic communication project.

Based upon the tasks you have identified, you can now construct the budget and the risk management plan. The budget is about how you are allocating and using the resources you have. For each task, you need to determine its cost. Cost is based upon the resources needed to complete a task. Your resources include personnel (work they do), materials, and equipment. Again, the budget is the cap for your costs. You must complete the tasks without exceeding your budget or you will have to make changes to your project to remain under your budget or find some way to increase the budget. Budgets can be linked with the project schedule to let you track spending along with the completion of tasks. That way at any point in time you can quickly determine if you are on time and on, over, or under budget.

Risks are uncertainties that can increase costs, or slow the execution of tasks. Severe weather, for instance, might delay the arrival of resources thereby causing a task to take longer to complete. Once you have your project schedule completed, the team should brainstorm possible risks associated with your tasks and timeline. For each risk, determine the likelihood of it occurring and the impact of its occurrence on the strategic communication project. For the risks with the highest combined likelihood and impact, create response options for the risk—what you will do if the risk occurs. Your options include eliminating risky elements of the strategic communication project or replacing risky elements with less risky ones, allowing more time for risky tasks, or allocating more resources to risky tasks to cover the potential contingencies the risk creates. For instance, you know that the printing and delivery of the T-shirts for the 5K race is variable due to demands on the printer you use and shipping time. You cannot eliminate the risk because you need the T-shirts. One option is to move up the date for ordering the T-shirts but that affects your cut-off date for registration. Another option is to spend more money for expedited shipping to speed up the delivery date of the T-shirts. At the very least, you are aware of the risk and prepared to cope with it. You can then update the project schedule based upon your risk-management plan.

Deliverables

Your deliverables are what you have produced at the end of the planning stage. First, you should have defined the target segments and the media for reaching them. You will know who you want to communicate with and the media you hope to use for communicating with them. The target segments are the key because they drive the other decisions made during planning such as the media selection. Second, you will identify your core message. This is your general theme and reflects the purpose of your strategic communication effort—what you are trying to say and do with the project. Third, you will complete your planning documents including the project schedule, budget, and risk-management plan. Keep in mind the documents may need to be revised as the project progresses. If anticipated risks occur, that can necessitate you altering the schedule and/or the budget. With planning completed, you are readying to begin the more exciting stage of communicating where you create the actual messages to be used in the project and sharing those messages with your target segments.

Running Example: Opportunity for Watford FC

Scanning noticed an opportunity with sensory rooms and research confirmed the opportunity for Watford management. The sensory room is to be built during the offseason because it involves renovations to the Vicarage Road Stadium. The sensory room will be completed one week before the Premier League season begins. Three days before the first home game, the private event for unveiling and dedicating the sensory room will be held. Management has allocated a generous budget for the event that will include catering. The strategic communication team has a date, a location, and the event. The private event will invite fans with ASD to be there for the unveiling and dedication of the sensory room.

The goal of the strategic communication effort is to enhance community perceptions of Watford FC—social approval of the organization. A sensory room is a way to demonstrate commitment to serving a variety of community segments. Your primary target segments will be local families in general with a special emphasis on those that have a member of the family with ASD. Your secondary segment will be local groups involved with ASD. There are two output objectives. First, "to have ten local families attend the unveiling and dedication of the Watford FC sensory room." Second, "to have two local ASD groups endorse the new Watford FC sensory room." Your primary objective relates to having people in the community aware of and utilize the sensory room. By having local ASD families tour the facility, you can increase the likelihood of them using the facility. Endorsements from ASD groups helps to enhance the community's social evaluation of Watford FC. You have two outcome objectives related to community social evaluations. Your first outcome objective is "to increase by 12 percent favorable views for Watford's contribution to the community among community members with families." Your second outcome objective focuses on the families who have members with ASD, "to increase by 25 percent perceptions that Watford is inclusive among active fans."

The core message of the event is "family." Watford FC has been built on the theme of family including the fans and community as part of the Watford FC family. The family theme will stress how Watford FC wants to broaden those who can be an active part of the Watford FC family through game-day experiences. The media will be a mix of owned, shared, and earned. The owned media will center on Watford FC web site (www.Watfordfc.com). Messages about the event along with images and videos of the sensory room construction will be posted to the team web site. Shared media will utilize the Watford FC Facebook page and @WatfordFC Twitter account. The earned media will target both traditional and digital channels. The tradition channels will include two local papers, the *Watford Hertfordshire* and *Watford Observer*, along with the national British Broadcasting Corporation (BBC). The digital channels will focus on the fan sites the WFC Forum (wfcforums. com) and Watford Mad (www.watford-mad.co.uk).

Here is a preliminary list of tasks for the event:

- Research and create a database of fans with ASD.
- Invite fans with ASFD and their families and request RSVP.
- Send a reminder to RSVP to fans and family.
- Monitor the RSVPs for those attending.
- Arrange for catering for the event (this will be done in-house).
- Arrange for event staff for the event including security, medical personnel, and people to greet guests.
- Train event staff in interacting with fans with ASD and their families
- Arrange for the manager, mascot, and select team members to attend the event.
- Research and create a database of local groups involved with ASD
- Invite leaders of local ASD groups and request RSVP.
- Send a reminder to RSVP local groups.
- Develop a program for the event.
- Print copies of the program.
- Create gift bags for attendees that contain team merchandise
- Decide on what team merchandise to include in the gift bag.
- Decide on a commemorative item for the event.
- Have the commemorative item produced and delivered.
- Create controlled media messages.
- Plan distribution of controlled messages.
- Execute the delivery of controlled messages.
- Create social messages.
- Monitor reactions to controlled messages.
- Plan the social message distribution (shared media).
- Execute the social message distribution plan.
- Monitor reactions to social messages.
- Create messages for soliciting earned media.
- Plan distribution of the earned media messages.
- Execute the delivery of the earned media messages.
- Monitor use of earned media messages.
- Identifying parking for attendees.
- Identify and secure the person who will host the event.
- Decide on an area for meet-and-greet with players, including photo taking.
- Create the hashtag for the event.
- Provide deals on the time and location of the event along with parking information and how people are to access the stadium.

As you look at the tasks, think about the possible dependencies between the tasks, the possible external dependencies, risks that must be considered, tasks that might need to be subdivided, and tasks that could be concurrent.

Running Example: Threat for the Los Angeles Dodgers

Scanning noticed a threat with anti-racism protests and research confirmed the threat for the Dodgers with the need to address concerns about systemic racism. The strategic communication effort will be rather simple and involved the release of anti-racism statements from the Dodgers. The strategic communication team needed to decide on the content and the timing of the anti-racism statements. The general goal of the anti-racism statements is to enhance social evaluations by positioning the Dodgers as an organization that was fighting systemic racism. The statements would include an action being taken by the organization to help fight systemic racism. The primary target segment would be the local community in and around Los Angeles because local support is important to sports teams. The secondary audience would be the global fan base of the Los Angeles Dodgers. The possible outcome objectives are related to the two target segments. Two possible outcome objectives for the local community could be: "To have 92 percent of community members concerned about systemic racism to approve of the statement" and "To have 85 percent of community members concerned about systemic racism to view the Dodgers as supporting efforts to end systemic racism." Racism is a polarizing issue. That is why the target segment for the two community objectives centers on those community members concerned about systemic racism. Two possible outcome objectives for fans could be: "To increase by 5 percent fan perceptions that the Dodgers are committed to diversity as part of the organization's corporate social responsibility efforts (CSR)" and "To increase by 3 percent fan approval of the Dodgers CSR efforts." Note the fan outcome objectives are more general and link the anti-racism statement to CSR. CSR is a critical element of an organization's reputation (Smith, 2012), hence, is an important factor for social evaluations.

The core message will center on Jackie Robinson because he links the Dodgers to past efforts to fight racism. Robinson faced a great deal of abuse as the first African American player in MLB. Robinson noted the need to "Stand Up" to racism. The core message here can be "Stand Up" to signal a continuation of the fight against racism. Another element of the core message needs to be support for Black Lives Matter (BLM), a driving force in the current anti-racism efforts. Recognizing BLM demonstrating an understanding of the current situation. The timing would be to release the messages on June 19 for the holiday, Juneteenth. Juneteenth commemorates when the last slaves were freed in the U.S. by Union troops arriving in Texas on June 19, 1865. Juneteenth creates a news peg (a reason to create a news story) for messages related to anti-racism.

The media would focus on the digital environment with a statement placed on the Dodgers' web site (owned) and a video posted to the Dodgers' Twitter account (shared). You also hope to attract the attention of the *Los Angeles Times* and online Dodgers fan sites (earned). The idea is that the digital content would attract the attention of the news media and social media users. As part of the message, the Dodgers will sell a special edition T-shirt. The proceeds from the sale of the T-shorts will help to support groups fighting for racial equality. The T-shirts represent an initial, small effort by the Dodgers to help fight systemic racism.

Here is a list of primary tasks for creating the messages:

- Prepare and get approval for the web site statement.
- Prepare and get approval for the Twitter video.
- Finalize the web site statement.
- Finalize the Twitter video.
- Release the message on June 19.
- Announce the messages on all Dodgers social media platforms.
- Get approval for the T-shirt design.
- Arrange a contract for printing the T-shirts.
- Arrange for shipping of the T-shirts.
- Create and test an online ordering and payment system for the T-shirts.
- Identify and partner with groups fighting racism.
- Provide information about the groups benefiting from the sale of the T-shirts.

As you look at the tasks, think about the possible dependencies between the tasks, the possible external dependencies, risks that must be considered, tasks that might need to be subdivided, and tasks that could be concurrent.

References

Barnhart, B. (2021). Social media demographics to inform your brand's strategy in 2021, Sprout Social. Retrieved from: https://sproutsocial.com/insights/new-social-media-demographics

Bundy, J., & Pfarrer, M. D. (2015). A burden of responsibility: The role of social approval at the onset of a crisis. *Academy of Management Review, 40*(3), 345–369.

Chen, J. (2020, March 26). The most important social media metrics to track, Sprout Social. Retrieved from https://sproutsocial.com/insights/social-media-metrics/

Coombs, W. T. (2005). Goals. In R. L. Heath (Ed.) *Encyclopedia of Public Relations* (pp. 364–365). Thousand Oaks, CA: Sage.

Deitrich, G. (2020, September 8). What is the PESO model? Spin Sucks. Retrieved from https://spinsucks.com/communication/peso-model-breakdown/

Dionisio, C.S. (2019). *Microsoft project 2019 for dummies*. Hoboken, NJ: John Wiley & Sons.

Foreman, J., & Argenti, P. A. (2005). How corporate communication influences strategy implementation, reputation and the corporate brand: an exploratory qualitative study. *Corporate Reputation Review, 8*(3), 245–264.

Heldman, K. (2009). *Project management professional exam study guide* (5th ed.). Indianapolis, IN: Wiley Publishing, Inc.

Hickman, T. M. (2015). The impact of fan identification, purchase intentions, and sponsorship awareness on sponsors' share of wallet. *Sport Marketing Quarterly, 24*(3), 170–182.

Laskin, A. V. (2016). Levels of evaluation: An agency's perspective on measurement and evaluation. *Public Relations Journal, 10*(2), 1–31.

Patanakul, P., Iewwongcharoen, B., & Milosevic, D. (2010). An empirical study on the use of project management tools and techniques across project life-cycle and their impact on project success. *Journal of General management, 35*(3), 41–66.

Pfarrer, M. D., Pollock, T. G., & Rindova, V. P. (2010). A tale of two assets: The effects of firm reputation and celebrity on earnings surprises and investors' reactions. *Academy of Management Journal, 53*(5), 1131–1152.

PMI (2014). The high cost of low performance, PMI. Retrieved from https://www. pmi.org/-/media/pmi/documents/public/pdf/learning/thought-leadership/ pulse/pulse-of-the-profession-2014.pdf

Smith, J. (2012). The companies with the best CSR reputations. Retrieved from www.forbes.com/sites/jacquelynsmith/2012/12/10/the-companies-with-the-best-csr-reputations/

Vos, M., Otte, J, & Linders, P. (2003). *Setting up a strategic communication plan*. Utrecht: Lemma Publishers.

7 Communicating
Creating the Final Messages

Many people are drawn to strategic communication because they are "creatives." Creativity in strategic communication should be about problem solving, not just crafting messages. Strategic communication is problem solving because it seeks to remediate a threat or leverage an opportunity. But most people in strategic communication think about creativity as developing the messages—the words and images that are shared with the target segments. Creativity becomes defined as making something. However, we should never lose sight of the problem-solving nature of creativity. Message creation occurs within specific parameters. You are not creating a message simply to express your inner artistic desires. Clients sometimes complain that some advertising agencies just try to express their creativity creating commercials that win design awards but do not solve the problem of selling products (Budimlija, 2017). Rather, you are creating messages that help to achieve specific objectives, appeal to specific targets, and fit within appropriate media channels. We are talking about strategic creativity.

Strategic creativity develops messages that address threats and/or leverage opportunities. Even though there are parameters, you must consider developing messages as your chance to express yourself and to be creative. Strategic communication is a mix of informative and persuasive messages with most being persuasive. So how do you develop effective, informative and persuasive messages? Part of that answer is you draw upon courses and personal experience with message development. This chapter provides some basic information about key points you should consider when developing strategic communication messages. We begin with the basics of informing others followed by persuading. The section on persuasion considers the general effects of source, messages, media/channels, and receivers. We then foray into visual communication with a discussion of data visualization and infographics. The chapter concludes with the deliverables for communication and the running case examples of threat and opportunity.

Touchstones for Strategic Communication Messages

A touchstone is standard for making a judgment. It allows you to determine the quality of some object such as a precious stone. A risk when

DOI: 10.4324/9781003031161-8

crafting strategic communication is drifting from the original intention of the messages as a person or team becomes lost in the creative process. Your objectives, target segments, and media channels are your touchstones for strategic communication. Regularly ask yourself if the messages you are creating help to achieve the objective, are appealing to the target segment, and are appropriate for the desired media channels. Referring back to your document will prevent you from drifting too far of course and creating messages that have no real connection to the first three stages of the strategic communication process. The research and planning stages have put you a course of action that should yield positive results for the organization. There are multiple ways of following that course of action—different message design options—but be sure you are still on that course of action.

Recommendations for Informing People

Informing people is about presenting new information in a way that makes sense to the audience. Your general goal is to create understanding. Clarity is critical when informing. The message must be free of jargon and use language the target audience can understand. The message also must be compelling to the target audience meaning they want to consume the message. You always write for the target segments, not yourself or your organization. You want the informative messages to resonate with the target segment. To resonate, the message must be relevant to the target audience. What do they get from attending to your message? People do want to know what's in it for them. Be sure to feature elements of your message that can offer some benefit to your target audience. How can this information benefit them or make their lives better in some way? On February 4, 2020, the Kansas City Sports Commission sent a digital message meant to inform fans of the Kansas City Chiefs. The message provided details about the parade and celebration of the Chiefs' Super Bowl victory. The event was called the Chiefs Kingdom Champion Parade. The details include the time of the event, the parade route (including a map), and the local of the rally following the parade. Fans of the Chiefs definitely want information about the Super Celebration and benefit by getting the details of how they can be part of the celebration from the informative message.

Informing is easier than persuading because people are less resistant to information than to persuasion. That does not mean informing is easy. In addition to clarity for comprehending a message and having content that resonates with the target segments, an informative message needs to compete for attention and remembrance with other messages. We are constantly bombarded by an array of messages every day. We ignore most through selective attention and remember even fewer through selective retention. Take advertisements as an example. How many advertisements do you actually attend to each day? Of those, how many do you actually remember who is selling the product? Two challenges for informative messages is to gain the attention of the target segment and to be memorable for them.

Attention depends on understanding your target segment. Visuals (still and video images), sound, and text can all catch our attention if it is something we find appealing. So, what types of visuals, sounds, or text (think headlines and hashtags) will appeal to your target audience? Sports fans enjoy inside information about a team or athlete. Visuals and text can be used to highlight that the message contains behind-the-scenes information. For headlines or hashtags, try to create an element of surprise or ask the audience a question. Again, the ideas in the headline or hashtag must have some appeal for the target audience. On July 11, 2014, LeBron James send a simple tweet: Homecoming. This message held great appeal of fans of LeBron James and the National Basketball Association (NBA). In one word, LeBron let fans know he was returning to play for the Cleveland Cavaliers. In this case the message was the headline and became a hashtag that held great appeal for all but the fans of the Miami Heat (LeBron's now former team).

Being memorable is closely related to gaining attention. People remember information that fills in personal knowledge gaps. People are likely to be interested in and remember messages that allow them to learn something new or helps them to improve their skills. An example would be a message that teaches people how to do something they are interested in such as improving a sports skill. Heath and Heath (2007) wrote a book about what makes ideas sticky. Sticky ideas are the ones people remember and share. The central theme needs to be simple. People should be able to easily identity and to repeat your central theme. Unexpected messages, ones that violate expectations are memorable. An example would be learning an odd fact about a sports team. Emotions can resonate with people and increase the memorability of a message. A message that captures the emotion of an important winning moment in a team's history would be memorable. When appropriate, a message should be told in a story format. A story has a plot, character, and an unfolding of action. Chapter 9 goes into much greater detail on storytelling. Keep in mind not all messages can be delivered in a story format. A flier or a tweet, for instance, are meant to be very simple and do not lend themselves well to the story format. Consider the digital message from the Kansas City Sports Commission about the Chiefs Kingdom Champion Parade. The message would probably be less effective if forced into a story format. People just needed to know how to be a part of the Chiefs Kingdom Champion Parade, not to read a story about the event. You need to understand your target audience to create a memorable message for them.

Recommendations for Persuading People

Persuasion seeks to have people voluntarily change their attitudes, beliefs, or behaviors. There are four key factors that can affect the persuasiveness of a message: 1) the source, 2) the message, 3) the media/channel, and 4) the receiver. In this section we summarize what decades of persuasion research tells about how to make a message more persuasive.

Source

The source is the person, group, or organization that is delivering the message. A source should be credible for the target audience. A credible source is an expert on the subject and is trusted. An attractive source is more persuasive than an unattractive source. Attractive means the source is appealing to the target audience (O'Keefe, 2016). For sports fans, players and mascots are attractive sources. Even coaches and owners might be attractive to fans. The attractive source can vary so team and strategic communication professionals need to know what sources appeal to their fans. The Dallas Cowboys, for example, frequently use the Dallas Cowboy Cheerleaders in their social media messages because of their popularity with fans. Homophily is a final source factor that refers to people finding people like themselves persuasive. A message from actual fans could be persuasive for sports fans because it is from people like themselves. More and more teams are using fan-generated content in messages reflecting the power of homophily. When Paul Rogers took over as the social media manager for AS Roma, he began using more fan-generated content because Rogers considers that to be the future of team social media content (Keaney, 2017). To use the power of the source in persuasion you must know who is credible, attractive, and/or similar to your target audience.

Message

For thousands of years, people have been interested in how the emotions and logic in messages affect people. Emotions can move people to action. For our purposes, it is better to think of emotions in terms of values. Values can evoke emotions. What values are important to your target audience and how can you use those values in your messaging? Does your target audience value family or belonging to a group? That knowledge would shape messages you create about the reasons for attending a live sporting event. Do you emphasize a family bonding experience or the chance to be with those who share your passion for the game?

Logic is about the arguments you create in the message—the reasons for doing something. People want evidence, reasons that support your argument, and not just to be told to do something. Two-sided arguments with refutation are a persuasive way to present messages based in logic. A two-sided argument recognizes there are reasons not to do what you are recommending. Refutation is providing reasons why the argument against your position should be rejected (O'Keefe, 2016). Some fans dislike the drinking and foul language at live sporting events. A two-sided argument with refutation could acknowledge that problem but indicate how that is not a concern in the "family friendly" section of the stadium or arena. You recognize the reason for not wanting to attend a live sporting event but refute the argument by offering an area where that concern no longer applies. A final concern related to logic is the use of explicit or implicit conclusions. Think of the conclusion as your call to action, what you want your target audience to do after consuming your message. Implicit allows people to draw their own conclusion from the message. The idea is that people are more likely to take the action if they figure out for themselves what you want them to do. Explicit directly tells the target segment what they should do. Research suggests implicit often fails because people draw the wrong conclusions from your message. Hence, the recommendation is to be explicit with conclusions by giving a clear call to action (O'Keefe, 2016). If you are trying to entice people to attend a game, the explicit message would be to state in the tweet some version of "you should come to the game." The implicit message would just laud the benefits of attending leaving the need to attend implied.

Be sure to give people enough information for acting on your call to action. That means including what is called mobilizing information. Mobilizing information is the precise information needed to take the desired action. Mobilizing information tells people when, where and how to engage in a behavior. Examples include the exact location of events, times and dates, directions to a location, links to web pages, and ways to donate. An example would be you are holding a youth workshop where members of your team will provide instruction about the team's sport to children aged 10 to 14 years old. People need to register for the event and then attend the event. The mobilizing information you would need includes: links to web page for registering for the event, the precise location of the event, the precise time of the event, directions to parking for the event, and anything the children need to bring with them for the event such as sports equipment. Box 7.1 provides an example of mobilizing information for an event held by the Pittsburgh Pirates. You may decide to have a small fee with the proceeds going to a local charity. In that case you would need to provide information on how to pay the fee such as payment through the team's web site prior to the event or collecting the fee the day of the event. Mobilizing information is about details. You cannot expect people to take action if they lack the information necessary to engage in that action.

BOX 7.1 Mobilizing information example

The 2020 PiratesFest, presented by Chick-fil-A Pittsburgh, will get underway at PNC Park with General Public access beginning on Saturday, January 25 from 11 a.m. to 5 p.m. Pirates Season Ticket Holders will have special access with the Pirates' Season Ticket Holders only night on Friday, January 24, from 4 p.m. to 8 p.m. and on Saturday from 9 a.m. to 11 a.m. prior to the General Public times.

The annual baseball carnival will have activities for the entire family featuring live events, free autograph sessions for kids 14 and under, prizes, games and the ability to purchase single-game tickets, ticket packages and groups for the 2020 season.

Throughout the event, Pirates players will be signing autographs in the Jim Beam Left Field Lounge for fans who secured tickets through the autograph ticket on-sale at **pirates.com/PiratesFest**.All proceeds from the autograph sessions will benefit Pirates Charities and their mission to support local nonprofits throughout the year.

Pirates Charities is encouraging fans to donate new youth baseball and softball equipment at PiratesFest to support local Pirates R.B.I. teams. Fans may drop off their new equipment or donate a suggested amount of $10 or more at the Service Tunnel entrance to receive a special Pirates wristband/headband. Pirates Reviving Baseball in Inner Cities (RBI) offers baseball and softball opportunities to more than 1,200 youth in local Pittsburgh neighborhoods in partnership with the Boys and Girls Clubs of Western Pennsylvania.

Parking Information

Parking lots and garages around PNC Park will be open for parking throughout the day including the North Shore Garage ($8), West General Robinson Garage ($8) and Red Lot 6 ($8), located across from PNC Park on General Robinson.

PNC Park Concessions

PNC Park Concession stands will be open on the Pittsburgh Baseball Club Level and in the Left Field Lounge area.

PNC Park Clubhouse Store

The PNC Park Clubhouse Store will be open throughout the day with great deals on Pirates merchandise.The store will also be set up in the Left Field Lounge with baseballs, autograph display cases and more. (PiratesFest, 2020)

Media/Channels

The early discussion of media and channels touched on this subject. Research has compared video messages to text and audio messages for persuasive effect.Video enhances the persuasive power of a favorable source (one that is highly credible or attractive). Text is easier to comprehend and better when the message is complicated. People can go back and re-read a text message (O'Keefe, 2016). Online, you can re-watch a video so text may have less of an advantage in that case.

Third party endorsement is another factor to consider with media channels. When others use your message, that other becomes a third-part endorser for your message. When a newspaper runs a story based upon information from a strategic communicator (publicity), the newspaper is endorsing the information by repeating it. The same holds true if an influencer uses information from a strategic communicator. Earned media always are considered to be third party endorsements. So are your social media posts that others choose to share with their followers. There is a belief that third party endorsements are more persuasive than paid media. For traditional media, there is little evidence to support that belief and in the digital world most people do not draw or perceive a difference between paid or earned. Still, influencers mentioning the information carries weight with their followers. Companies pay influencers millions because followers will "follow" their advice including buying products and services they like. But this is more a function of source attractiveness than a media or channel effect but does relate to third party endorsements. Keep in mind the results from using influencers is mixed. It is not uncommon to get no real effect from an influencer beyond exposure (Bobila, 2019). Carefully consider whether or not an influencer will help to achieve your larger organizational goals.

Receivers

The receivers are the target segments that consume your strategic communication message. Two factors relevant to receivers and persuasion is involvement and identification. Involvement is the potential connection between the target audience and your message. Instrumental involvement concerns how your actions can help the target audience to achieve a desired outcome. As we noted earlier, there needs to be something in the message for the target audience. Involved receivers examine the message carefully. This close examination will enhance the persuasiveness of powerful messages to change attitudes. Identification, as discussed earlier in the book, is when a person sees part of their own identify in the organization. People are more easily persuaded when they identify with a source (O'Keefe, 2016).

Identification is a critical factor when communicating with fans. Committed fans have a strong identification with the team or athlete. As a result, messages from the team or athlete can be very persuasive. Remember that committed fans are the ones most likely to buy the products from companies sponsoring a team. The connection between the team and the product is what sells the product. Chelsea Football Club sponsors include Yokohama Tyres and Carabao Energy Drink. That means if a Chelsea fan needs new tires they might buy Yokohama or reach for Carabao when they want an energy drink. That means you have a built-in advantage when communicating with committed fans. However, there are times when you are trying to reach new or potential fans. In those cases, you do not have your identification edge and will have to work harder to persuade these target audiences. That is when it is critical to feature the desirable outcomes the target audience get from taking the actions you are requesting. People must understand how they benefit from taking the desired course of action. For instance, existing fans want to be at live sporting events but the potential fans need reasons to be there to overcome their many reasons for not attending live sporting events. Fans need to desire the social environment promised by attending a live sporting event.

Visual Communication

The visual aspect of a message has always been important because of the power of visuals. Visual is considered the most powerful sense and is linked to grabbing attention, aiding recall, and making something memorable (Dunlop & Lowenthal, 2016). Some have argued we are a visual society making visual literacy and visual communication an essential skill (Estrada & Davis, 2015). Visual literacy is "the ability to interpret and create visual messages" (Dunlop & Lowenthal, 2016, p. 42). Visual communication is the process of people using visual symbols to intentionally send a message for others to consume (Estrada & Davis, 2015). For our purposes we are talking about still and video images that communicate messages to our target segments. We see the ideas of visual communication in strategic sports communication as sports teams embrace visually oriented social media channels such as Instagram and TikTok.

Generally, visuals help us to understand and to remember information. Visuals have at least six basic uses. One, visuals can be used to explain a complex process or concept. Two, visuals can provide a quick overview of a topic. Three, visuals can be used to display research findings. Four, visuals can be used to summarize a long report. Five, visuals can be used to compare and to contrast options. And six, visuals can be used to raise awareness of a topic (Nediger, 2019). It is helpful at this point to shift from a general discussion of visual communication to more specific applications of visual communication that are relevant to strategic sport communication.

Data Visualization

Data visualization is the graphic representation of information and data. Data visualization has been around for centuries. You have experienced and probably created data visualization without even knowing it. Graphs and charts are data visualization techniques. Each take data or information and present it visually for the message consumer. Box 7.2 presents an overview of the different types of charts and graphs. Column graphs present lines vertically while a bar chart presents the lines horizontally. Both types of charts are useful for comparing categories or to show changes over time. A pie chart helps to show part-to-whole comparisons such as how money in a budget is spent. A doughnut graph does the same type of part-to-whole comparison but with a different layout. Line graphs are used to show changes over time and are effective ways to

---

BOX 7.2 Different types of charts and graphs

Column Chart: useful for comparing values
Bar Chart: useful for comparing values
Pie Chart: useful for displaying percentages or showing part of the whole
Doughnut Chart: useful for showing parts of a whole
Line Graph: useful for showing values over time

---

show trends of volatility in data such as stock prices. Excel is one of the common software programs that allows you to create graphs and charts. Data visualization is ideal when you need to reveal patterns or trends in data (Nediger, 2019).

Infographics

Infographics are the "new" element of visual communication rising to prominence in about 2010. An infographic is "a larger graphic design that combines data visualization, illustrations, text, and images together into a format that tells a complete story" (Kim, 2014, p. 6). An infographic tells a complete story. A story has a plot and characters. Think of the structure and organization of the infographic as the plot because it conveys what you are trying to accomplish with the message. This plot will describe the relationship between various points, think of these points as the characters. An effective infographic illustrates how the various points relate to one another—tells a story.

Researchers have been studying what makes an effective infographic. Effective means people are drawn to, understand and remember information from the infographic. The two key factors for an effective infographic are coherence and resonance. Coherence means there is logic, clarity, and consistency in the design. Coherence is a function of planning. You must make sure each element in the infographic has a clear purpose and serves to advance your story. Resonance is about the message connecting with your target segment. We have mentioned before how a message needs to resonate with the target segment. That means people perceived the relevance of the message to their own lives. Think about a message that resonated with you. What about that message attracted you? Resonance is a function of research and planning because it requires a detailed understanding of the target segment (Dunlap & Lowenthal, 2016). Box 7.3 provides a list of questions you can ask yourself when constructing an infographic to determine how you are doing with coherence and resonance. Always remember, you design the message for the target segment, not for the organization.

BOX 7.3 Questions to ask before creating and infographic

Message design experts asking a series of questions before developing an infographic to ensure that the infographic development is worth your time and effort (Dodge, n.d.; Leibtag, 2012).

1. Does it add value for people and help to achieve organizational goals?
2. Can you present complex data into an educational graphic?
3. Does the infographic have a clear call to action—urge people to do something?
4. How long will the information be relevant?
5. Does the infographic fit with existing content?
6. Is the infographic unique or does it repeat existing information?

Dunlap and Lowenthal (2016) use Duarte's work on visual representation to categorize infographics into six categories. These six categories are useful ideas for thinking about the structure and organization of an infographic. A flowchart is used to show a process or can be modified and become a timeline. Flowcharts are perfect to illustrate a process such as how to buy and use digital tickets. It also can be used for a timeline that shows the key points in the history of a team, information commonly found in what is known in strategic communication as a backgrounder. Structure is used to the classification of concepts. You might use an infographic to show the various types of fans for the team as part of an internal presentation to other managers in the organization. Cluster is used to show the grouping of relationships. You might want to show how the different types of fans are related to one another in your internal presentation. Radiate shows the connections between things. You might show how the team is connected to various local charities or community groups as part of a community relations message. A pictorial shows realistic concepts. There are times you want to show images of real people or places in your infographic. This might involve using actual images of a mascot or the stadium in an infographic. Display is used for comparison and contrast or to show cause and effect. You might use an infographic to compare various ticketing options for fans or to show the financial effect of the team on the local community. Obviously, you do not have to choose only one of the six but can mix elements of the six in your infographic. The categories are simply a way to understand the various ways you might use an infographic.

You only use visual communication when it serves a purpose. Visuals are chosen because of their relevance to the message, not as mere decoration. Always ask yourself, "Why are we using this visual element?" If you do not have a good answer, do not use the visual element. A good answer is the visual element, say a shape or a color, attracts attention while a bad answer is it looks pretty. Visuals should complement any text and not overpower the text. Just as bad delivery can hurt the content of a presentation, a bad visual can hurt the content of a message. Infographics are appealing because research tells us people are more likely to consume an infographic than a message that is text only (Nediger, 2019). However, research also tells us that "an infographic is not appropriate for all messages" (Dunlap & Lowenthal, 2016). Think about how an infographic can help to achieve your objective and works for the target segment being targeted in your strategic communication effort.

The current visual society and visual nature of many social media platforms demand we consider the role of visual communication within common strategic communication tactics drawn from public relations. Clearly most social media platforms are designed to utilize visuals (still and/or video) and the use of visuals enhances fan engage on social media (Montgomery, 2019). The challenge is still finding the correct visual to complement the message. Let us consider some of the more traditional public relations tactics and how data visualization and infographics might work with them. Brochures, backgrounders, and fact sheets are prime candidates for visual communication. Brochures might benefit from a graph or chart. Moreover, the information on the brochure might be amenable to becoming an infographic. We find similar applications for backgrounders and facts sheets. Backgrounders provide historical information about the company and biographies of executives. Fact sheets are often long, running three to five pages in length. The historical information about the company would work well as a timeline (flowchart) infographic. Similarly, the biographies of executives are stories that can include a pictorial element with images of executives and cluster that shows the organizational relationship between executives. A fact sheet provides the essential information about a product, service, person, or event. Review the information on the fact sheet to see if it can be converted to infographic. Again, the information must be appropriate for an infographic to benefit from the advantages one provides for attracting message consumers.

Not all organizations have the need for position statements. However, the Blacks Lives Matter movement in 2020 proved that situations may arise where organizations are compelled to make a position statement. During this time, organizations found it a necessity to have a position statement on racism in the U.S. Polling data found that people expected organizations to speak about race. Moreover, people were likely to punish organizations that remained silent and reward those organizations providing thoughtful, anti-racism statements and actions. (Edelman, 2020). Position statements articulate the organization's position on an important issue such as deregulation or immigration. Position papers are likely to increase in importance in the near future because stakeholders now expect organizations to take stands on various issues, especially social issues such as same-sex marriage and the climate emergency (Arenstein, 2020; Porter Novelli, 2020).

A position statement can be long because it includes background information on the issue, actions the organization is taking on the issue, and actions people can take on the issue. Longer documents often have executive summaries for people who want the short version. An infographic is one way to provide a summary of your organization's position statement. An infographic would be used in addition to the position paper and not a replacement for it. Issues are complicated and demand a more detailed document for those stakeholders wanting to know more about the issue, the organization's position on the issue, and the actions the organization is taking to resolve the issue. The tradition press release is a poor fit with infographics and data visualization and generally is declining in use. However, the social media release (SMR) should be augmented with digital features such as links to additional information. Visuals can be used to augment an SMR as well. Data visualization could be used to provide summaries of data and information. You are unlikely to create an infographic version of an SMR unless the content was a nice fit with the format. The key is to think about if and how visual communication can be used to enhance the strategic communication you are creating.

Summary

In one chapter we cannot provide all the information you need to know about message creation. There are hundreds of books written about informing, persuading, and using visual communication. This chapter provides a few highlights to give you an idea of the factors you should be considering when developing messages. Creating messages requires that you to draw upon knowledge from beyond this book and the class that uses it. You will take ideas from other classes, experiences, internships, and jobs to craft strategic communication messages.

Deliverables and Delivery of Messages

Your primary deliverable will be the final messages you plan to use in the strategic communication effort. You should compile a final list of the messages along with when and where (media/channel) the messages will be delivered to your target segment(s). Your planning schedule will have this basic information, such as milestones. You are just adding in the finalized messages. You can then begin to monitor reactions to these messages as they are delivered. If there is a quick, negative reaction to any messages, you need to consider changes to your planning schedule and potentially a need to re-think the messages or even the objectives of the strategic communication effort. The next chapter on evaluation will provide more details on how to monitor and how to assess your strategic communication efforts.

Running Example: Opportunity for Watford FC

At the communication stage, the core messages become the actual messages distributed to the target segments. While the early stages presented hypothetical information about the sensory room strategic communication effort, the actual message delivered by Watford FC is presented here:

> Watford FC is delighted to announce the opening of a new Sensory Room, which will enable children on the autism spectrum to enjoy match days in a calm environment.
>
> Watford are proud to be the first club in the south of England to open a Sensory Room, which will also be the largest of its kind and only the third permanent facility in the country.
>
> As a club with a proud family tradition, the pioneering opening of the room is set to have a big impact on children who struggle to cope with big crowds and noise levels at the stadium.
>
> The room is managed by fully-trained staff with a background in working with children on the autism spectrum and is accessible from Vicarage Road.
>
> Theo Canter, the six-year-old son of Upper Graham Taylor Stand season ticket holder Andrew, has so far been unable to enjoy matches with his Dad and older sister Ruby. Theo and his family became the first Watford fans to use the room at the recent match against Everton and thoroughly enjoyed their day.
>
> "We are so delighted that the Watford FC Sensory Room is now a reality," said Andrew.
>
> "We have been incredibly impressed by the Club's receptiveness and dedication in ensuring these facilities have been made available. The Sensory Room will make a huge difference to Theo and we look forward to coming along to more matches."
>
> (Sensory, 2017)

Notice how family is central to the message and that there is an endorsement from a fan and father of a son who is on the autism spectrum. This message was posted to the Watford FC web site.

Questions to consider:

1. How might Watford FC adapt the message for posting on the team's social media platforms?
2. What makes this message a good fit with the target segment(s)?
3. What might be done to improve the appeal of the message for the target segment(s)?

Running Example: Threat for the Los Angeles Dodgers

As with the opportunity running example, actual messages from the Dodgers' announcement are presented here. The first message is a statement made by the team:

> "As an organization, we take our responsibility of community leadership seriously and know that our core values of collaboration, communication,

respect and diversity will mean nothing unless we act on them now," said Stan Kasten, Dodgers president and CEO.

"In commemoration of Juneteenth, we've asked our team to use Friday to create a space for reflection, action and engagement to advance racial equity. Most importantly, we want everyone to consider how each one of us can continue to work together towards a better future."

On Friday, the club released through its social media platforms a video pledging "to heed Jackie's call" and step up the fight against racial injustice because "Black Lives Matter."

The club is working on several upcoming initiatives, including the conversion of a current fundraising effort that benefits COVID-19 relief efforts to also support organizations that combat racial inequality.

The Dodgers and the Los Angeles Dodgers Foundation are selling special edition T-shirts that can be purchased at **dodgers.com/together**, where information on the beneficiaries can be found.

(Gurnick, 2020)

The Los Angeles Dodgers posted the following Tweet and long with a video: "We listen, we learn, and we unlearn. We renew our purpose and we take action." The video included the following statements that appear as text within the 1:40 video:

On April 15th, 1947, Jackie Robinson became the first Black man to play Major League Baseball in modern history.

But as the past few weeks have reminded us, the progress that he envisioned has not yet been realized.

Jackie once said, "Life is not a spectator sport, it you're going to spend your whole life in the grandstand, just watching what goes on, in my opinion, you're wasting your life."

It's time to heed Jackie's call and STAND UP! We must get out of our seats and be more than just spectators.

Although the institution of slavery has ended, it was replaced by systems of extreme injustices, legal discrimination and institutionalized violence across generations of Black Americans that have continued to this day.

We the Los Angeles Dodgers will not stand by idly ignoring the evils of racism and social injustice.

THE TIME IS NOW.

BLACK LIVES MATTER.

(Los Angeles Dodgers, 2020)

We can see how the messages were built around Jackie Robinson and the need to stand up against racism.

Questions to consider:

1. How would you evaluate the choice of the Dodgers to use text in the video?

2. How well do the messages fit with the target audience?
3. What potential do you see for backlash against the messages?
4. How would you evaluate the choice to center the message on Jackie Robinson?

References

Arenstein, S. (2020, June 10). The complexity of brands taking a stand at this time, PRNEWS. Retrieved from https://www.prnewsonline.com/stand-brands-diversity

Bobila, M. (2019, July 26). Wake up, sheeple: Brands are losing money off of fake influencer followers, Fashionista. Retrieved from https://fashionista.com/2019/07/fake-influencer-fraud-report-2019

Budimlija, V. (2017, June 20). How the art world is inspiring new visions of marketing data, Campaign. Retrieved from https://www.campaignlive.co.uk/article/art-world-inspiring-new-visions-marketing-data/1436979

Dunlap, J. C., & Lowenthal, P. R. (2016). Getting graphic about infographics: Design lessons learned from popular infographics. *Journal of Visual Literacy, 35*(1), 42–59.

Estrada, F. C., & Davis, L. S. (2015). Improving visual communication of science through the incorporation of graphic design theories and practices into science communication. *Science Communication, 37*(1), 140–148.

Gurnick, K. (2020, June 19). Dodgers celebrate Juneteenth, urge action, Los Angeles Dodgers. Retrieved from https://www.mlb.com/dodgers/news/dodgers-celebrate-juneteenth-close-offices

Heath, C., & Heath, D. (2007). *Why some ideas survive and others die: Made to stick.* New York: Random House.

Keaney, M. (2017, October 18). AS Roma head of digital, Paul Rogers, LinkedIn. Retrieved from https://www.linkedin.com/pulse/social-influencer-head-digital-roma-paul-rogers-mark-keaney

Kim, D. H. (2014). A case study of infographics for national defense-focusing on the data journalism of Afghanistan war in Guardian. *Spatial Information Research, 22*(5), 43–52.

Los Angeles Dodgers (2020). Juneteenth, Twitter. Retrieved from https://twitter.com/Dodgers?ref_src=twsrc%5Egoogle%7Ctwcamp%5Eserp%7Ctwgr%5Eauthor

Montgomery, E. (2019, February 11). How to use visuals effectively for social media marketing, Three Girls. Retrieved from https://www.threegirlsmedia.com/2019/02/11/how-to-use-visuals-effectively-for-social-media-marketing/

Nediger, M. (2019, October 30). Presentation design guide: How to summarize information for presentations, Venngage. Retrieved from https://venngage.com/blog/presentation-design/

O'Keefe, D. J. (2016). *Persuasion: Theory and research* (3rd ed.). Los Angeles: Sage.

PiratesFest highlights for Friday, January 24 and Saturday, January 25, 2020 at PNC Park (2020, January 22). MLB. Retrieved from https://www.mlb.com/press-release/press-release-piratesfest-highlights-at-pnc-park?t=pirates-press-releases

Porter Novelli (2020, June). The business imperative for social justice today. Retrieved from https://www.porternovelli.com/wp-content/uploads/2020/06/PN-Purpose-Tracker_Business-Imperative-for-Social-Justice-Today.pdf

Sensory room: A guided tour (2017). Watford FC. Retrieved from https://www.watfordfc.com/club/sensory-room-guided-tour

8 Evaluating

Assessing Success or Failure and Learning

In the discussion of planning, we noted a project/strategic communication effort must be on time, on budget, and of sufficient quality. Assessing if your strategic communication effort is on time and on budget is relatively easy. You simply determine if you met the deadline and if you stayed on budget. The on time and on budget answers are simply "yes" or "no." Sufficient quality is a much more complicated question. Our explanation of evaluation examines the many ways there are to assess the quality of the strategic communication effort by focusing on the objective(s) you created during planning.

You have invested time and money in your strategic communication effort. Now you need to know the return on investment (ROI) which answers the question: "What did we get for our money?" As a strategic communication professional, you should want to validate the effects of your work. Moreover, others in an organization would like to know what strategic communication is doing to help the organization. Evaluation is critical to being accountable and demonstrating strategic communication's contribution to the organization. Measuring the success or failure of your strategic communication is half of evaluation. While evaluation is the last step in the strategic communication, it is not the end of the process. The second half of evaluation is learning. Through evaluation you improve future strategic communication efforts. You will learn what worked well and why along with what did not work and why. Evaluation helps you to understand the strengths and weaknesses in your scanning, research, planning, and communication stages. For instance, your evaluation might prove the value of a particular social media platform or uncover problems with understanding and moving a particular target segment.

Think of evaluation as the step that unites all the other steps. Your scanning and research created the information necessary for you to plan (objectives are essential to evaluation), to create, and to disseminate your messages. But was the opportunity really beneficial and did you have the proper information? You answer the broader question of "Did you effectively leverage an opportunity or mitigate a threat?" Evaluation helps you to understand what you did well and not so well during the entire strategic communication effort. While we visualize the strategic communication as a process with one

DOI: 10.4324/9781003031161-9

step following another, we need to remember that every step in the strategic communication process is related in some way to every other step in the process. Evaluation allows you to take stock of your actions during the complete strategic communication process. This chapter is a review because it draws upon the other four stages in the strategic communication process. The central focus of evaluation involves objectives and the need to consider larger organizational goals in evaluation.

Evaluation and Objectives

Without proper objectives, you cannot execute evaluation. Objectives provide your standard of success by specifying what should occur when the target segment is moved by your messages. Metrics are an essential element of evaluation. A metric is a quantifiable measure used to track and to assess the status of a process. A variety of metrics are used when assessing objectives. In this section we revisit the types of objectives and types of change to understand how each relate to evaluation. The three types of objectives create three levels of evaluation: output, outreach, and outcome.

Output and Outreach

Output and outreach objectives are related to assessing the process of the strategic communication effort. One function of output objectives is to determine if you executed all the tasks you had identified in your planning schedule. It answers the question, "Did you do everything you intended to do?" Reviewing the output objectives should be done during the strategic communication effort as well as at the end to make sure you do not miss a task. You also can review the tasks to see how accurate your time and cost estimates were. Such data allows you to improve the accuracy of your task estimates in the future thereby improving the planning process. For instance, getting a permit for an outdoor event might be one of your tasks. You might discover that permit can take six days to be approved but the actual time is really 15 days. You can then adjust your time estimates for securing permits in future strategic communication efforts.

The outreach objectives allow you to assess if and how gatekeepers used your messages. It is simple to determine if an influencer mentioned your organization, product, or service after you contacted them. You would use the established methods for determining if a media outlet used a news release and how it used that information. Mentions is a basic social media metric that identifies when an organization, product, or service appears in the media, a blog, or social media post. Share of voice (SOV) is frequently used along with mentions. The SOV is the amount of coverage of your organization compared to your competition. Share of impression (SIV) is a variation of SOV that examines the percentage of the total number of people who might be exposed to your mention compared to your competitors (Pecánek, 2020). But you need to move beyond the simple use a message to how the information was used. You need to determine if your core message was captured in the messages created by the gatekeepers. There is a concept known as message pull through. A core message is pulled through when the gatekeeper repeats the key ideas from your core message. Let's say you sent a message about an upcoming promotion your team designed to be family-friendly. Family-friendly is the core message because you want to cultivate families attending games. You have message pull-through if gatekeepers create messages that reflect your family-friendly theme. We need to remember that outreach objectives are means to an end. You want the gatekeepers to relay your message so that your target segments will be affected, which is an outcome objective. Similarly, sentiment helps to determine if the message was used as intended. You hope your message triggers a positive message by the gatekeepers and sentiment determines if a message is positive, neutral, or negative.

Knowledge change fits with both output and outreach objectives. Typically, an awareness change is part of a larger effort to change attitudes or behavior rather than the final outcome for a strategic communication effort. If you use owned media, the knowledge objectives are more output. Did you actually create and disseminate the messages? If you used earned media, the knowledge objectives are more outreach. Did the gatekeepers use your messages as intended? Knowledge change can include assessments of exposure (your target segments encounter the messages), attention (your target segments notice the message), comprehension (target segments understand the message), and retention (the target segments remember the message) (Wilcox, Cameron, Reber, & Shin, 2013). For example, people need to be aware of the blood drive before then can donate blood. You might assess awareness of the blood drive as a way to assess the effectiveness of reaching the target segments (an output) and their recall of that information. This would let you know if the target segments were exposed to and remembered your message. However, it does not provide insight into whether or not they acted on that information. Remember you can conduct some of this assessment in planning and communication stages such as testing comprehension of the message.

Outcome

The outcome objective is what you hope to achieve through the strategic communication effort. It is about moving people in some way. Outcome objectives seek to change people through attitudes, behavior, or some combination of the two. Ideally, the changes not only achieve your objectives but contribute to the larger organizational goals of revenue generation and/or social evaluation. We need to consider how you might assess the various outcome objectives.

We will start by considering evaluation of behavior outcomes because the ultimate goal of strategic communication is to move people to action. As Don Stacks (2002), a renowned expert in strategic communication research noted, "The behavioral objectives are often what 'count,' and they in the end define the success or failure of a campaign" (p. 29). The first consideration for evaluation is if the outcome objective is seeking to hit a target amount or a specific change. A target amount could be the number of people attending an event, amount of money raised by a charity auction, or amount of blood donated during a blood drive. A target amount does not require any pre-effort measurement, you simply count your desired target behavior. If your objective is a percentage change, such as increase donations or attendance by 10 percent, you need a pre-effort assessment along with an assessment following your current strategic communication effort. Any change must be measured against some original standard such as the amount donated the previous year. You must be able to compare the desired behavior to some existing amount if you want to show change in that behavior. Conversion is another measure of behavior. Conversion is when a person clicks a link in your message to access a specific web page or an event like a webinar. Obviously, you are hoping that accessing that information leads to additional behaviors, such as buying a ticket or merchandise, but conversion does show you have moved the target segment to some action.

Social evaluations such as reputation are forms of attitude because they relate to how people assess your organization. Assessing attitudes requires survey data to understand how people perceive the organization. Again, if your objective involves a percentage change, you will need pre- and post-effort assessments. If you intended your community relations event to improve perceptions of the organization benefitting the community by 5 percent among people living near the stadium, you need to assess community perceptions of the organization before and after the strategic communication effort for that community relations event. Box 7.1 provides some sample outcome objectives and how you might collect the data necessary to assess them. The key in evaluation is that there is a logical connection between the data you collect and the objective you are assessing. It should be clear that the data really do reflect (measure) the objective. Moreover, do not think the output and outreach assessments demonstrate the effectiveness of your strategic communication effort. Only outcome objectives serve as true markers of success or failure for your strategic communication effort.

BOX 8.1 Sample objectives and evaluation options

To increase annual community blood drive contributions by 12 percent.

You have a specific target amount for this year's blood drive. Count the number of pints donated this year and compare it to the number collected last year.

Larger organizational goal: social evaluation related to social responsibility.

Examine traditional media for stories about the blood drive and assess the sentiment analysis of the stories. Your hope is to generate positive stories.

Examine your social media posts about the blood drive for comments and assess the sentiment analysis of the comments. Your hope is to generate positive posts.

Run a simple poll on Twitter to get an idea what percentage of the respondents felt the community blood drive improved people's assessment of the organization's social responsibility.

Ask those donating blood to complete a short survey. Ask the people who contributed how they found out about the blood drive to see which media attracted them to the blood drive. This will help you make future decisions about media use for blood drives. Ask people their motivations for donating blood. You can use the information in future messaging about the event. Ask people how strongly they support the team to determine if there is a connection between fan identification and blood donation.

To increase ticket sales during the preseason from Instagram posts by 8 percent.

Larger organizational goal: revenue.

You are using your Instagram account to help create ticket sales. You develop a new strategy this year designed to be more effective than the previous year. You can then compare the number of ticket sales generated last year compared to the same time period this year. Ideally your total will show an 8 percent increase.

Review the engagement numbers (Likes, Comments, and Re-posts) for the Instagram posts designed to sell tickets. Compare those engagement numbers to those received by the messages the previous year. Ideally the engagement number this year will be higher suggesting greater interest in this year's messaging.

Review the Instagram ticket sales post comments for sentiment analysis to determine if people are reacting favorably or unfavorably to the posts.

The social media data gives you some insight into how well or poorly the posts are resonating with your target.

Conduct focus groups of people following the team on Instagram. Ask questions about the posts used to sell tickets to get a more detailed understanding of what people liked or did not like about the messages.

To have 150 children participate in skills development day.

To increase the amount of money raised by the annual 5K fun run by 10 percent.

To increase fan engagement on Instagram by 20 percent.

To generate 25 conversions for the new partial season ticket plan.

The Larger Organizational Goals

In addition to the strategic communication objectives, your strategic communication effort should help to achieve the larger organizational goals of revenue generation and social evaluation. Social evaluations are linked to revenue. Positive social evaluations enhance revenues while negative social assessments typically erode revenues (Roulet, 2020). Moreover, revenue generation and social evaluations are very broad goals and you can be more specific in your evaluation. For instance, your strategic communication effort might target ticket sales, merchandise sales, perceptions of the team's contribution to the community, or perceptions of the team's stance on a social issue. The point is there are different ways to specify the organizational goals. What is critical is that you link your evaluation to these goals in some way.

You need to think about what data you can collect that will show a link between your strategic communication effort and revenue and/or social evaluation. Let's consider two examples to illustrate the possible connections between strategic communication objectives and organizational goals. In the first example, your strategic communication effort sought to increase fan engagement on your Instagram account by 12 percent. Your data indicates you reached your target objective, so how does that relate to revenue? First, you can monitor ticket and merchandise sales before and after your strategic communication effort. Moreover, you can provide links from the new Instagram messages to ticket and merchandise pages. If sales increase and you can show conversion through the new Instagram messages, you can argue that your strategic communication effort played a role in increasing those sales. Clearly other factors might also be affecting sales, but the conversion strengthens the argument that your messages are at least part of the reason for the increase. Second, by enhancing engagement numbers and perhaps even total followers, your Instagram account becomes more attractive to your sponsors. Engaged fans are a desirable target segment for sponsors because research shows those fans buy the products of sponsors. You could then use the new engagement numbers to attract sponsorship deals that include your Instagram account.

The second example involves improving perceptions among people living near the stadium of the team's contribution to the community. This is a specific form of social evaluation. People living near your stadium are impacted by your operations. Those impacts include traffic, parking, and noise. A supportive as opposed to an angry community is a significant difference when you need to make changes that will affect them or when a team asks a community for assistance related to infrastructure. The social approval facilitates the changes and reduces their costs while social disapproval makes the changes more difficult and more costly. Social evaluation is a long-term investment but one that is worth making. A positive change in the team's social evaluation is a larger organizational goal, not just a strategic communication objective.

Part of your evaluation needs to make the case for why the strategic communication efforts contributes to larger organizational goals. As Wilcox, Cameron, Reber, and Shin (2013) stated, "The ultimate objective of any public relations effort, as has been pointed out repeatedly, is to accomplish organizational objectives" (p. 133). You must be able to demonstrate how strategic communication is contributing to the organization. Proving your value is easier when you incorporate thinking about organizational goals throughout the strategic communication effort and collect evaluative data that allow you to argue for how strategic communication contributes to revenue and/or social evaluation.

Deliverables

At the end to the evaluation stage, you should be able to produce a report that includes the assessment of the overall success or failure of the strategic communication effort, the contribution to organizational goals, and lessons learned for improving future strategic communication efforts. Points one and two are the most important to others in your organization because they relate to ROI for strategic communication. The assessment of success of failure must feature your outcome objectives(s), the data used to assess the objectives, and the rational for why the data demonstrates success or failure. Data never speaks for itself, which is why you need to explain how the data relates to your objectives. This can be done in an executive summary and does not require pages and pages of text. You might even create an infographic to display your results. You should link the strategic communication evaluation to the larger organizational goals. Again, specify the organizational goals, the data you collected, and how the data supports your position that the strategic communication effort contributed to the larger organizational goals.

The third point about learning is for the benefit of the strategic communication team. This is a much longer document that includes output, outreach, and outcome objectives and their assessment. You want details because that will help the strategic communication team improve future efforts. The team can build upon what worked and find ways to improve upon what did not work. For example, if a message did not resonate with the target segment, future strategic communication efforts might need better research on the target segment or try different values that might resonate more with the target segment. This is an opportunity to look at the strengths and weaknesses of your entire strategic communication process. If the strategic communication team aims to improve, they must know what they do well and what they do not do so well. Keep in mind this is not about assigning blame, but a means of improving the performance of the entire team. If your evaluation becomes a search for blame, it will create a negative climate and preclude learning from the evaluation effort.

Conclusion

Evaluation is about accountability for strategic communication. It is a chance to prove the value of strategic communication to the organization by demonstrating its ROI. You prove your value to the organization by demonstrating how strategic communication contributes to larger organization goals when it achieves the specific objectives of a strategic communication effort. In addition, evaluation gives insights into the other four stages. The strategic communication team learns what aspects of scanning, research, planning, and communication are working well and which need improvement. Evaluation should be treated as a learning experience, not a way to blame people for failures or mistakes. Think of evaluation as a positive experience, not as something to avoid or dread. Even a failure is an opportunity to learn and to improve your strategic communication skills.

Running Example: Threat for the Los Angeles Dodgers

The evaluation begins by determining if the strategic communication effort was on time and on budget. That is simply checking completion and costs. The outcome objectives for the community were: "To have 92 percent of community members concerned about systemic racism to approve of the statement" and "To have 85 percent of community members concerned about structural racism to view the Dodgers as supporting efforts to end systemic racism." A survey is required to assess if community members approve of the statement and perceive the Dodgers as supporting ending systemic racism. The survey would be sent to a random sample of people living in the Los Angeles area. The survey includes a qualify question to determine whether or not the respondent is concerned about structural racism. You would include those respondents who express an interest in structural racism because the message is unlikely to resonate with people who do not care about the issue. In-depth interviews with community members would provide additional, qualitative data. In-depth interviews explore people's perspectives on an idea or situation, in this case the anti-racism message from the Dodgers. The details from the in-depth interviews could help to explain why people approve or disapprove of the statement and if the statement does create the impression of the Dodgers fighting systemic racism.

Finally, the data from the Twitter post should be analyzed. Review all comments to determine if the sentiment in negative or positive and for any themes emerging from the comments that indicate how people feel about the message. A strong positive sentiment and favorable themes in comments are more evidence of the positive reception of the message. Also check the applause rate and compare it to previous CSR-related tweets to see if the ant-racism message was generating more or less applause than a typical CSR-related tweet. Check the average engagement rate and conversation rate for the post to see if it generated more or less engagement and conversation than other CSR-related posts. Ideally, the tweet outperforms previous CSR-related tweets to provide another indicate the positive reception of the message. Also review the social media conversion rate for the Twitter post as it relates to the sale of the T-shirts. A strong social media conversion rate is evidence of the value of the tweet.

A similar approach could be used to assess the two outcome objectives for fans: "To increase by 5 percent fan perceptions that the Dodgers are committed to diversity as part of the organization's corporate social responsibility efforts (CSR)" and "To increase by 3 percent fan approval of the Dodgers' CSR efforts." A team should be tracking fan perceptions of the team repeatedly over time using either a panel of fan or a random sample of fans. It is through such data that a team can identify changes in social evaluations such as reputation. Because CSR is a key component of social evaluations, teams should collect data about fan perceptions of CSR efforts regularly. The evaluation would compare fan perceptions of diversity and approval of CSR efforts before and after the release of the anti-racism statement. The evaluation effort should include addition questions in the post-strategic communication survey about if the fan knows about the statement and how they learned about the Dodgers' anti-racism statement. By comparing the responses of those who knew about the anti-racism statement and those who did not, you have a clearer idea if exposure to the statement moved perceptions of diversity and approval of CSR efforts more than lack of exposure to the message. If people who were exposed to the anti-racism statement reported the Dodgers were more strongly committed to diversity and approved of the CSR efforts than those not exposed to the anti-racism statement; you can make a stronger argument for the positive effect of the anti-racism statement on social evaluations of the Dodgers. In-depth interviews would be a useful addition to probe more deeply into how people perceived the anti-racism statement and ow that affected their perceptions of the Dodgers' diversity and CSR efforts. You would check *The Los Angeles Times* for any news stories and if fans' sites mention the tweet to assess the outreach objective.

Lastly, the surveys and in-depth interviews should contain questions about exposure and media. It is useful to know if a respondent was exposed to the anti-racism statement and how the respondent learned about it. As noted earlier, exposure can be used to compare the social evaluations of those who know about the statement to those who did not know about it. Ideally, those that were exposed will have more positive social evaluations of the Dodgers thereby showing the value of strategic communication. Exposure rates give you a sense of how well or poorly the media mix was at reaching your target segments. For those who were exposed, knowing the media they used to learn about the message gives you useful information for refining how you might reach these target segments in the future. Finally, the strategic communication team conducts a debrief session where they assess what went well and what could have been improved. The notes from the debrief can be used to improve future strategic communication efforts.

Running Example: Opportunity for Watford FC

The initial assessment of the strategic communication effort involves determining if you are on time with the project and not over budget. These are simple assessments. The evaluation then moves with your two output objectives. It is easy enough to determine if ten families agreed to attend the sensory room dedication and if two community groups endorsed the sensory room. Securing these endorsements should enhance perceptions of the club. The outcome objectives were: "To increase by 12 percent favorable views for Watford's contribution to the community among community members with families" and "To increase by 25 percent perceptions that Watford is inclusive among active fans." The outcome objectives each require pre- and post-strategic communication assessment. Surveys would be your main source of data to make the comparisons to determine if favorable views of Watford contributing to the community among those with families and if fan perception of Watford inclusivity with fans improved by the desired amount. You would check the two local newspapers for stories to assess your outreach objective.

Focus groups could be conducted with the target segment to explore in more detail how they feel about the sensory room and the effect the sensory room has on perceptions of Watford FC. You can combine the quantitative data from the surveys and the qualitative data from to document the success of failure of the strategic communication then make the connections between this data and the effects on social evaluations of Watford FC. You explain how the data you have collected supports improved social evaluations. The survey data can document improvements in specific evaluations among the target segments. The focus group data provide specific examples of how people connect the sensory room to more favorable perceptions of Watford FC. The data from the fan perceptions is critical to making a case for the strategic communication effort having a positive effect of the team's social evaluation because fans are a key target segment for social evaluations.

The social media metrics can provide additional insight about the performance of the social media posts. Social media comments also should be evaluated to determine if there is a favorable reaction to the sensory room. Carefully review the comments to determine if the family theme is reflected in the comments—the family theme is resonating with people. Check the applause rate, average engagement rate, and conversation rate for the sensory room messages. Compare those results to previous CSR-related posts to determine if the sensory room posts were performing at average, below average, or above average for a CSR-related post. Social media is a part of most strategic communication efforts meaning social media metrics should be part of your evaluation process.

Part of the post-strategic communication assessment includes if people heard about the sensory room and through which channel(s) they experienced the message. You should conduct awareness and media usage for most strategic communication efforts as part of the output assessment. This additional information helps with learning more about the effectiveness of various channels for reaching this target segment. The strategic communication team conducts a debrief session where they assess what went well and what could have been improved. Notes from the debrief can be reviewed for lessons that could improve future strategic communication efforts. Be specific about the lessons such as if a particular vendor was unreliable or provided exceptional service. Specificity is what makes the debrief information useful to improve future strategic communication efforts.

References

Pecánek, M. (2020, August 13). What is share of voice? How to measure it across channels. Retrieved from https://ahrefs.com/blog/share-of-voice/#:~:text=You%20monitor%20keywords%20(brand%20names,to%20the%20overall%20market%20mentions.

Roulet, T.J. (2020). *The power of being divisive: Understanding negative social evaluations.* Stanford, CA: Stanford University Press.

Stacks, D.W. (2002). *Primer of public relations research.* New York: Guilford.

Wilcox, D.L., Cameron, G.T., Reber, B.H., & Shin, J.H. (2013). *Think public relations.* New York: Pearson.

9 A Transmedia Narrative Transportation (TNT) Approach to Strategic Communication

An Alternative Perspective

The strategic communication process presented in Chapters 4 through 8 is commonly used in public relations, marketing communication, and advertising (Anderson, 2019). It is a well-established and proven means for developing strategic communication efforts. But does that mean it is always the best option? We say the answer to that question is "No." Strategic communication has changed drastically with the advent of the digital environment. Stakeholders and organizations have a much wider array of digital platforms for communicating with one another. Moreover, these new digital platforms present greater opportunity for interaction between stakeholders and organizations and stakeholders with other stakeholders. The evolution of communication channels does not mean the established framework for strategic communication obsolete. But it should make use question if there are new, alternative perspectives for developing strategic communication efforts. In this chapter we present the transmedia narrative transportation approach as one alternative to the established framework for developing strategic communication efforts presented in the previous five chapters. The chapter begins with the value of being agile in strategic communication and the pressures on strategic communication to become more agile. The focus then shifts to explaining the transmedia narrative transportation approach, how it is agile, and how it can be applied to strategic sports communication.

Being Non-linear: Agile Strategic Communication

In 2015, Van Ruler began arguing that organizations needed to become more agile in their communication. The traditional model of strategic communication, outlined in the preceding chapters, was not enough for modern practitioners. This traditional model of strategic communication was very linear and rigid with its focus on objectives. Strategic communication needed to be more agile and focus on creating and sharing meaning with stakeholders. An agile approach is a new mindset premised on formative research and guided by continuous monitoring. Strategy is still central to an agile approach just executed differently by practitioners. The focus is on organizational goals (generalized ends) instead of specific objectives. Strategy is emergent rather than planned. The reality is most planned strategy has

DOI: 10.4324/9781003031161-10

emergent elements. Plans change as strategic communication professionals face reality when they implement their plans and things do not do as "planned." Strategy is a pattern rather than a specific movement from point A to point B to point C (Van Ruler, 2015).

Managers still have a target. Say we want to get to point C. However, how we get to point C is variable. We may go A to B to C or perhaps A to F to G to C. The point is that strategy provides a direction and an outcome but how managers reach that outcome emerges from interactions with stakeholders. An agile view of strategic communication realizes that stakeholders can be actively involved in shaping the pattern that emerges as managers pursue their goals. Strategic sports communication involves fans who are often very active meaning an agile view of strategic communication makes sense as an option for developing strategic communication efforts.

Trends Pressuring Strategic Communication to Become Agile

The agile approach to strategic communication does not completely replace the linear model. Rather, strategic communicators have options for how to pursue goals through strategic communication. There are four interrelated trends in strategic communication that push strategic communication professionals towards an agile approach: 1) digital channels, 2) storytelling, 3) stakeholder engagement, and 4) co-create meaning. It is important to understand how these trends create pressure for agile strategic communication and their specific relevance to strategic sport communication.

Digital Channels

Social media platforms and web sites provide a variety of digital channels that can connect organizations and stakeholders. More importantly most stakeholders are now digital naturals, people willing and able to embrace digital channels (Young & Åkerström, 2015). The problem is that strategic communicators have been slow to really leverage the interactive nature of digital channels (Coombs, Falkheimer, Heide, & Young, 2015). Just read any article about how organizations are using a specific social media platform and the results are the same—no true interaction. The lack of interactivity is problematic in strategic sports communication because you have fans who want information and want to connect with players and teams. Fans do embrace digital channels for sports communication much more so than consumers of other products or services (Pegorano, 2014)

Storytelling

If you read practitioner writings to keep up on the field of strategic communication, you have noticed a keen interest in storytelling. In fact, you have been told that strategic communicators are actually storytellers (e.g., Dziuban,

2016). It is great to see practitioners embrace storytelling because communication researchers have long recognized the power of stories and storytelling (Burke, 1969; Fisher, 1985; Heath, 1992). Stories serve as magnets to attract people to content and to encourage them to consume that content. Storytelling is about creating compelling content. As Paul Rogers, head of digital communication at football club AS Roma, has observed, "content is great or it's not." Great content resonates with fans (Keaney, 2017). Storytelling is one means of building great content that will resonate with fans.

Stakeholder Engagement

Both digital channels and storytelling have hinted at the idea of stakeholder engagement. The essence of stakeholder engagement is interactions that seek to improve understanding between stakeholders and organizations and stakeholder with other stakeholders. Engagement is used in many different ways ranging from simply stakeholders reading messages to stakeholders being involved in organizational decision making (Ashley & Tuten, 2015; Taylor & Kent, 2014). Interaction is the key concept in engagement. "Interaction is central to engagement because the parties must share their ideas, perspectives, expectations, and experiences if they are to learn from one another" (Coombs & Holladay, 2018, p. 384).

Fans do seek engagement with athletes and teams. A good example of that are the Twitter accounts of athletes (Pegorano, 2014). Athletes have no problem gathering followers. Cristiano Ronaldo has over 76 million followers while Neymar Jr has over 44 million and LeBron James over 43 million followers. Even with so many followers, athletes tend to utilize a limited form of engagement. Only a small percentage of athlete tweets are interactive reflecting a true social interaction with fans (e.g., Fredrick, Lim, Clavio, & Walsh, 2012). Tweets and retweets can be social or parasocial. Social tweets and retweets demonstrate true interaction. A tweet will be in direct response to another user or a retweet with commentary. Parasocial is more one-sided where there is just a tweet or a retweet without commentary (Kassing & Sanderson, 2009). Parasocial interaction (PSI) is a concept from media research where fans develop relationships with media figures, including television characters. Fans feel as if they are in a relationship even though there is no real interaction with the media figure or character (Kassing & Sanderson, 2010).

In most cases the tweets reflect a form of parasocial interaction. The athlete is posting content, even questions, that generate reactions from the fans. However, there is very little athlete response to the fan reactions. For instance, an athlete will post a question to fans, the fans post answers to the question but the athlete does not respond to those answers. Fans seem to like and to embrace the parasocial interactions and are satisfied with parasocial relationships with athletes (Fredrick, et al., 2012). Fans are engaging with the parasocial content when you assess Twitter engagement with common indicators such as likes, retweets, and comments.

Co-creating Meaning

The co-creation of meaning is one mechanism for trying to achieve improved understanding between stakeholders and organizations. Co-creation of meaning is also a way to enhance firm value (Hatch & Schultz, 2010). Co-creation of meaning tries to get stakeholders and organizations on the same page by helping them to interpret situations and events similarly (Heath & Coombs, 2006). Coombs and Holladay (2018) argue that co-creation of meaning is about valence:

> We know multiple parties will not co-create the exact same meaning for an event or situation due to various perceptual biases. However, multiple parties can agree that event or situation is either good or bad. Though the parties may have different reasons for their assessment of valence, the key is that the parties agree on the valence.

For instance, when a sports team sponsors a local charity 5K race, the idea is to co-create the meaning that both the team and its stakeholders view the sponsorship as positive.

It is important to note that strategic sports communicators do not give meaning to their stakeholders. Rather, meaning is social constructed as the various parties engaged in communication must agree on what the situation or event means for them. In the 5K race example, stakeholders must interpret the sponsorship as favorable to align with meaning the team is hoping to share. Again, the stakeholders and the strategic communicators do not need to share the exact same meaning. The team could place value on the sponsorship because it bolsters the view that the team supports the community while stakeholders might like the charity that benefits from the run or simply enjoying running in a 5K race. The point is regardless of why people like the event, there is a shared positive valence for the 5K. How people interpret an event, an action, or a situation is essential to strategic communication.

Strategic sports communication is shaped by the larger trends that are affecting strategic communication. The four pressures identified in this section all favor the use of an agile approach to strategic communications. Strategic sports communicators must be aware of the pressure to use digital channels, to tell stories, to engage stakeholders, and to facilitate the co-creation of meaning. We agree with others who believe these four trends/pressures move strategic communicators towards a more agile approach to their jobs.

The Transmedia Narrative Transportation (TNT) Approach to Strategic Communication

Now that we understand pressures to be agile, the question is "How do we create strategic communication in an agile manner?" One way to create agile strategic communication is through the transmedia narrative transportation

(TNT) approach. The TNT approach is both tactical and strategic. The TNT approach uses transmedia storytelling as its tactical focus and narrative transportation theory for its strategic guidance. This section explains transmedia storytelling, moves to narrative transportation theory, then concludes by explaining how the two combined to form the TNT approach including what makes it an agile approach to strategic communication.

Transmedia Storytelling

Have you ever seen one of the Marvel movies, a *Star Wars* movie, or *Game of Thrones*? If your answer is yes, you have experienced transmedia storytelling. Transmedia storytelling occurs when multiple voices (people) tell multiple but related stories through different channels. Henry Jenkins (2006) used the term transmedia storytelling to capture how the entertainment industry uses various people to create multiple, related stories through film, books, graphic novels, and video games. Think of transmedia storytelling having four characteristics. First, there are multiple storytellers as different people are telling various stories. Second, the stories are united by a common storyline known as the storyworld. The storyline is the overarching story arc that gives us information about characters and plots that serves to define the boundaries of the storyworld. Third, the stories appear in multiple media meaning people use a mix of channels and not just one channel to tell the stories. Fourth, the same story is not simply told in each media, each story and channel must be able to add something unique to the storyworld. An example would be a book based on a movie. If the book simply retold the movie, it is not transmedia. While the book and movie have some overlap, the book must give us insights in plot and characters that we could not experience in the movie to be transmedia storytelling.

Star Wars is the best example of transmedia storytelling. There are nine primary movies and two related movies in *Star Wars*. There are hundreds of books and graphic novels about various *Star Wars* characters. There are multiple animated cartoon series and soon-to-be-released live action television programs involving *Star Wars*. The movies each provide new information and insights into the characters and advance the plot. Similarly, the books, graphic novels, and various television shows reveal information we would not otherwise know about characters and events in the *Star Wars* universe. There are a wide array of voices telling *Star Wars* stories through various channels. The risk with transmedia storytelling is fragmentation. The storyworld is a buffer against fragmentation by providing some means of keeping consistency between the various stories and storytellers. When Disney bought Lucasfilm and the *Star Wars* franchise, one of the first steps it took was to establish the storyworld that would govern all future *Star Wars* stories (Gonzales, 2016). The Disney storyworld now defines what is part and what is not part of the official *Star Wars* universe.

People are already applying ideas from transmedia storytelling to public relations (Capriotti & Kuklinski, 2012; Gill, 2015; Sutherland & Barker, 2013,

2014) and marketing communication (Bourda, 2014; Tenderich, 2013). This demonstrates the potential value transmedia storytelling has for strategic communication. The limitation with transmedia storytelling is that it tends to be descriptive of practices with little theory. This means that transmedia storytelling is overly tactical, hence it needs to be combined with theory to give a stronger strategic focus. The TNT approach fuses transmedia story-telling with narrative transportation theory.

Narrative Transportation Theory

As noted earlier, people have long known the power of stories. Think about how we read stories to young children to build their imaginations. One reason for the power of stories is the ability of a story to transport a person to another place. A person becomes a traveler when they engage with a story and their journey to another place can change them (Gerrig, 1993). Research in narrative persuasion has found that visiting another place in a story can change attitudes, beliefs, and intentions that reflect those portrayed in the story (Green & Brock, 2000). An example would be a person reading a story about the dangers of plastic straws for sea turtles and deciding to no longer use plastic straws. Stories can persuade people by influencing their affective and cognitive responses. Even consumer attitudes and cognitive responses can be affected by engaging marketing stories (Van Laer, DeRuyder, Visconti, & Wetzels, 2014). Stories draw their power not from the analytic dimension of persuasion that results from a careful and critical analysis of a message. Rather, narrative transportation emerges from the draw of the story. A story can change people when the mental imagery evoked in a story facilitates people internalizing elements of the story.

We begin the explanation of narrative transportation theory with its four central terms: storyteller, story, story receiver, and narrative. The storyteller is the person who creates and tells the story. A story can be an account or simply a sequence of events created by the storyteller. Plots, characters, a climax, and an outcome are the key elements of a story. The story receiver is person or persons consuming the story by interpreting the story. Narrative describes how the story receiver interprets the story. While the story is created by the storyteller, the story receivers have agency because they create the narrative by interpreting it through their own biases. The narrative is an active process of interpretation by the story receiver.

Van Laer et al. (2014) identified the process of narrative transportation is their analyses of narrative transportation theory research. Narrative transportation begins when people choose to process a story. Next a story receiver must be transported into the story through mental imagery and empathy. Finally, the story receiver must lose track of reality during transportation. Not all stories will transport people and not all people are transported by any one story. Stories vary in their power to transport people and people vary in their general predisposition to be transported (Van Laer et al., 2014). We can assess where a story transported a person by using the narrative transportation scale. This scale allows you to assess the degree of narrative transportation experienced by the story receiver (Green & Brock, 2000). The narrative transportation scale can be used in pretesting stories and to assess how a sample of your target audience is responding to the story.

As strategic communicators, your job is to create the most compelling story—a story that will transport people. Three factors have been identified as important for creating compelling stories: 1) imaginable plots, 2) identifiable characters, and 3) verisimilitude. Imaginable plots have details that provide cues to stimulate the formation of mental images from a story. Identifiable characters are ones that story receivers can relate to thereby creating empathy for the character. Verisimilitude refers to whether or not people find the story believable and lifelike. Verisimilitude is "the likelihood that story events may actually happen" (Van Laer et al., 2014, p. 802). The story receiver needs to believe the story could happen if the story is fiction. For instance, a team builds its campaign for the new season around the story of the team winning the league title. If the team has no realistic chance of winning the title, the story lacks verisimilitude. Fans will identify with the team and the story can have the cues and details to stimulate their imaginations but the story will ring as untrue thereby precluding narrative transportation.

The story receivers naturally vary in their ability to be narratively transported. Furthermore, various factors affect the intensity of a person's narrative transportation. Familiarity is when a person has previous knowledge about or personal experience with a story or the genre of the story. Familiarity enhances story processing and makes it easier for mental images to be created. When people focus their attention on a story, narrative transportation is more intense (Van Laer et al., 2014). The outcomes from narrative transportation include various persuasive effects including an increase in story-consistent affective responses, a decrease in critical thought, an increase in story-consistent beliefs, an increase in story-related attitudes, and an increase in story-related intentions. If people are narratively transported by a story, the story receivers develop beliefs, attitudes, and intentions similar to those expressed in the story (Van Laer et al., 2014). For instance, if a story explains how attending a sporting event together increases familial bonding, people should believe attending a game is beneficial to a family, have a more favorable attitude toward attending a game, and express a stronger intention of attending a game. Strategic communicators can use familiarity and attention in efforts to bolster the narrative transportation potential of their stories and the potential persuasive effects of those stories.

Theory is valuable to strategic communicators because theory indicates why a certain course of action should be effective. Narrative transportation theory provides strategic guidance for the use of stories for persuasive effects. The TNT approach fuses the tactical aspects of transmedia storytelling with narrative transportation theory to create a unique perspective for creating strategic communication efforts. The next section explains how the TNT approach can be used by strategic sports communicators.

The TNT Approach Applied to Strategic Sport Communication

The storyworld is the core in the TNT approach to any form of strategic communication. The storyworld unifies the diverse communication created by the TNT approach. This means the storyworld provides rules about what is and is not part of the storyworld. Strategic communicators must craft storyworlds that inspire other people to contribute their own voices to the storyworld through a variety of media. Storyworlds must be flexible and permit others to add their own stories (and voices) through a range of media. For any organization, the larger organizational goals are a potential source for storyworlds. Organizational goals will reflect the mission and purpose of an organization. The mission is what an organization is trying to accomplish while the purpose is why the organization is trying to accomplish those goals. Most organizational missions express a desire to be successful. For sports organizations, success is about attracting fans and generating revenue. Purpose is about the way an organization creates personal meaning for people and is socially beneficial.

Mission and purpose work together rather than being in competition with one another. Patagonia is a great example of mission and purpose working together. Patagonia makes quality products that consumers purchase but do so in an environmentally friendly manner. For instance, Patagonia stopped making pitons, metal spikes used in climbing, because pitons are environmentally unfriendly. Patagonia's management took the action even though selling pitons was very profitable. Patagonia also switched to organic cotton because that was environmentally friendly even though it raised the price of Patagonia's clothes (Cook-Degan & Bronk, 2018). It is helpful to think of mission and purpose as the values that present an organization's identity— who managers believe the organization to be. Values are an excellent foundation for a storyworld. The value becomes the boundary for what can and cannot be in the storyworld while allowing flexibility because people can vary in how they interpret a specific value such as freedom or inclusion.

A specific example will help to illustrate how mission and purpose can provide material for crafting storyworlds. The Premier League is a highly successful football organization in the UK that includes top teams such as Manchester City, Liverpool, and Chelsea. The mission of the Premier League is "to stage the most competitive and compelling league with world-class players and, through the equitable distribution of broadcast and commercial revenues, to enable clubs to develop so that European competition is a realistic aim and, once there, they are playing at a level where they can compete effectively" (Statement, 2019, para. 1). Note the general mission is competitive and compelling play which connects to revenue generation. The Premier League also has a statement of principles which reflects purpose. The principles are important because they shape the way the Premier League "think, communicate and behave with each other and the world around us" (Principles, 2019, para 1). No harassment or discrimination and desire to create a safe and inclusive environment for fans are part of the

Premier League principles. From the mission and principles, a strategic communicator for the Premier League could distill values to be used in creating a variety of storyworlds. For instance, the Premier League could construct a storyworld around the problem of discrimination and the value of non-discrimination.

The TNT approach fits the four trends that affect strategic communication. The TNT approach is predicated upon storytelling and demands the use of multiple channels. Social media platforms fit nicely with the TNT approach. A number of corporations use social media as a central part of their TNT approaches for communicating social responsibility (Coombs & Holladay, 2018). Narrative transportation requires that people engage with the story content. Moreover, transmedia storytelling encourages people to apply ideas from the stories to their own lives and to share messages with others (Jenkins, 2006). Engagement is an integral element for the TNT approach. Co-creation is reflected in how stories are persuasive and the emphasis on people adding their own stories to the storyworld. A story is persuasive only when those consuming the story share similar emotions and attitudes with characters in the story. If the story consumer does not co-create meanings in the story similar to the story creators, there is no persuasive effect from the story. Story consumers (story receivers) should be encouraged to be story creators as well. Story consumers help to co-create the storyworld by sharing their own stories—adding more voices to the storyworld. The storyworld is a collaborative effort and not the sole dominion of the organization that originated the storyworld.

It is the collaborative nature of the storyworld that makes the process non-linear and dependent on emerging strategy. The strategic communicator (storyteller) starts the process by presenting an initial version of the storyworld. The initial message outlines the basic values of the storyworld, explains how others can join the communication process, and encourages people to add their own voices to the storyworld. The initial message simply provides a general direction for people, not a specifically planned route for them. As more people add to the storyworld with their stories and comments, a strategy will emerge as everyone begins to see where the messages are going. The strategic communicators for the organization begin the process but stakeholders move the process forward. Strategic communicators will provide additional messages to stimulate the process, but the content (stories) created by the stakeholders ultimately decide the final direction of the communication effort.

Evaluation is challenging because the strategic communicators cannot have specific objectives, just general goals. Assessment needs to capture the intended outcome—the general direction the strategic communication was anticipated to go. Because strategy is emergent, strategic communicators also must try to capture the unintended consequences. What unexpected ideas and actions emerged that would be relevant for evaluation? Finally, the process itself. The TNT approach demand engagement by stakeholders. Any type of engagement should be considered a valuable result, not just what the organization hoped might occur (Coombs & Holladay, 2018). Consider all engagement a form of feedback that can inform the organization–stakeholder relationship. Finally, strategic communicators must find ways to link the outcomes to the organizational goals the strategic communication efforts was designed to address.

Let's return to the Premier League and its value of anti-discrimination. One manifestation of discrimination is racist chants by fans. This problematic fan behavior hurts the team in many ways including potential penalties resulting in lost revenue and discouraging some people from becoming or remaining fans of the team. The Premier League could create an anti-discrimination storyworld for a communication effort. This anti-discrimination effort would provide an opportunity to engage fans, in a constructive manner, on the topic. A new section could appear on the Premier League web site that announces a new anti-discrimination campaign intending to reduce racist chants. The core of the storyworld could be personal stories from various Premier League players who have been subjected to abusive chants due to their race or religion. The stories would be a mix of written narratives and videos from the players. The stories would convey the harmful effects of these chants, highlight lessons learned from the stories, and discuss actions fans could engage in to reduce the behaviors. In addition to the web site, the Premier League would begin a Twitter feed dedicated to discrimination concerns, have links to various resources for those affected by discrimination, and offer in-person training about coping with discrimination in various venues including sport, school, and the workplace.

Stakeholders would be engaged by asking them to contribute their personal stories about the negative effects of discrimination in sport and in their person lives. Again, the stories could be written or videos. The stories would be curated by the strategic communication team. This means select stories would be featured on the web site along with expert commentary about lessons that could be learned from the stories and the offering of new training session designed to address the new discrimination concerns that emerge. The stories provided by the stakeholders determine the general direction of the new content and topics appearing on the web site. No one can anticipate the stories that will be submitted and what aspects of discrimination will be explored in the stories. The Twitter feed would provide updates on anti-discrimination efforts and encourage fans to report cases of abuse they have seen at matches. People also could post questions or topics of concern they would like to raise about discrimination. Polls could be taken about the suggested topics leading to future materials for the web site and social media efforts. Again, the stakeholders determine the exact direction of the communication effort through their concerns and polling results. The concerns would be answered by experts providing another form of engagement with stakeholders.

Evaluation could focus on the amount of people engaging with the anti-discrimination effort. This would include the number of answers to Twitter questions, comments on stories, likes, retweets, people attending trainings, and number of stories submitted to the web site. An unintended consequence could be the need to create new anti-discrimination polices for the Premier League. The strategic communication effort could reveal and overlooked problem that requires the League's attention. The idea is to learn from the process and to engage stakeholders, not be overly focused on specific objectives. The Premier League also could track the number of incidents of racist chants. If the number of racist chants trend down after the communication effort has progressed, this would be evidence of reaching the organization objective about anti-discrimination. A survey of fans could be conducted as well before the communication effort and at various intervals after the communication effort begins to track perceptions of behaviors they consider inappropriate. If fans to increasing perceive racist behaviors as problematic, this is addition evidence the larger organizational goal is being achieved.

For the past few years, Chelsea Football Club (Chelsea FC) in the Premier League has been involved in an antisemitism communication effort. The effort is a result of a lingering antisemitism problem with some Chelsea fans that is directed primarily at supporters of Tottenham Hotspur. Tottenham is another team based in London, like Chelsea, and historically has support from the Jewish community. The Chelsea antisemitism campaign fits the characteristics of the TNT approach. The antisemitism effort uses multiple channels including videos, web sites, lectures, and in-person training. Many of Chelsea's star players have been featured in the online videos and appear at events with fans designed to raise awareness about antisemitism. Chelsea has invited two different Holocaust survivors, Mala Tribich MBE and Harry Spiro, to talk to the team and to share their experiences via video with Chelsea fans. Chelsea FC referred to Spiro's talk as teaching about the Holocaust with him sharing his story and the stories of his family. The in-person training involves going to primary schools to discuss antisemitism and a special educational program for fans found to have been involved in antisemitic behavior. This last component is unique to Chelsea. Most problematic fans are banned for life from attending matches. The owner of Chelsea, Roman Abramovich, is Jewish and believes education can help to rehabilitate these problematic fans.

In January of 2019, after an antisemitic incident at a match, ten different Chelsea fan groups joined to form the antisemitism effort with the label #ChelseaTogether. The fan groups included Chelsea Supporters' Trust, Chelsea Pride, We Are the Shed, and The Chels podcast. These fan groups utilized a variety of social media platforms to disseminate the message including the Twitter feed @TogetherChelsea. Here is how the fan groups explain their effort:

> We are Chelsea Together. We are fans united by a desire to end all forms of discrimination in and around the Chelsea Football Club. Regardless of race, gender, sexual orientation, religion, age or disability: we are Chelsea; and we are together.
>
> (Chelsea Together, 2019)

Chelsea FC embraced the effort but did not formally integrate these fan efforts and stories into their official campaign. Here is the statement for Chelsea FC: "We wholeheartedly welcome the #ChelseaTogether initiative from Chelsea supporters which is further evidence the vast majority of Chelsea fans want to see all forms of discrimination kicked out of the game, wherever they may occur" (Chelsea, 2019).

The Chelsea antisemitism strategic communication effort is transmedia because multiple voices are sharing various stories through a variety of media. The stories from the two Holocaust survivors provide powerful narratives to create awareness of the problems of antisemitism and to promote changes in beliefs, attitudes, and intentions. The communication effort is weak on engagement beyond the training efforts. The web site and online videos do not stimulate much engagement because people are not asked for comments or to share their own stories. Chelsea FC is too controlling of the message making the effort more linear than non-linear. The Chelsea antisemitism effort is a minimal application of the TNT approach that could more fully embrace the interactive elements of the approach including linking the fan efforts with the team-initiated effort.

Conclusion

The TNT approach is not appropriate for every strategic communication effort. There is room in the strategic communicator's toolbox for both linear and non-linear strategic communication approaches. The TNT approach is both tactical and strategic with the storyworld as its centerpiece. In situations when a storyworld can be constructed and there is a desire to engage stakeholders, the TNT approach is a great option. Storyworlds are built from the values that comprise organizational goals, missions, and purpose. Strategic communicators must be willing to allow the strategic communicative effort to evolve through stakeholder engagement. The sports organization might initiate the communication effort and set a general direction, but the contributions of the stakeholders creates the emergent strategy that guides the communication effort. Because fans have a strong desire to engage with sport, the TNT approach is an excellent fit with strategic sports communication for some strategic communication efforts.

References

Anderson, L. N. (2019). Teaching the introductory public relations course: Pedagogical recommendations. *Journal of Communication Pedagogy, 2*(1), 58–62.

Ashley, C., & Tuten, T. (2015). Creative strategies in social media marketing: An exploratory study of branded social content and consumer engagement. *Psychology & Marketing, 32*(1), 15–27.

Bourda, M. (2014). This is not marketing. This is HBO: Branding HBO with transmedia storytelling. *Networking Knowledge: Journal of the MeCCSA Postgraduate Network, 7* (1). Retrieved from: http://www.ojs.meccsa.org.uk/index.php/netknow/article/view/328/160.

Burke, K. (1969). *A rhetoric of motives*. Berkeley, CA: University of California Press.

Capriotti, P., & Kuklinski, H. P. (2012). Assessing dialogic communication through the Internet in Spanish museums. *Public Relations Review, 38*(4), 619–626.

Chelsea FC (2019). Retrieved from: https://twitter.com/hashtag/chelseato gether?lang=en.

ChelseaTogether (2019). Who we are. Retrieved from: https://twitter.com/ togetherchelsea?lang=en.

Cook-Degan, P., & Bronk, K. C. (2018). Want a purpose-driven business? Know the different between mission and purpose. Retrieved from: https://www. fastcompany.com/40552232/want-a-purpose-driven-business-know-the-difference-between-mission-and-purpose.

Coombs, W. T., Falkheimer, J., Heide, M., & Young, P. (2015). *Strategic communication, social media and democracy: The challenge of the digital naturals*. London: Routledge.

Coombs, W. T., & Holladay, S. J. (2018). Innovation in public relations theory and practice: A transmedia narrative transportation (TNT) approach. *Journal of Communication Management, 22*(4), 382–396.

Dziuban M. (2016). The power of storytelling in PR. Retrieved from: http://www. cision.com/us/2016/03/the-power-of-storytelling-in-pr/ .

Fisher, W. R. (1985). The narrative paradigm: An elaboration. *Communications Monographs, 52*(4), 347–367.

Frederick, E. L., Lim, C. H., Clavio, G., & Walsh, P. (2012). Why we follow: An examination of parasocial interaction and fan motivations for following athlete archetypes on Twitter. *International Journal of Sport Communication, 5*(4), 481–502.

Gerrig, R. J. (1993). *Experiencing narrative worlds: On the psychological activities of reading*. New Haven, CT: Yale University Press.

Gill, R. (2015). Why the PR strategy of storytelling improves employee engagement and adds value to CSR: An integrated literature review. *Public Relations Review, 41*(5), 662–674.

Gonzales, D. (2016). The current, canonical Star Wars timeline. Retrieved from: https://www.geek.com/culture/the-current-canonical-star-wars-timeline-1683840/.

Green, M. C., & Brock, T. C. (2000). The role of transportation in the persuasiveness of public narratives. *Journal of Personality and Social Psychology, 79*(5), 701–721.

Hatch, M. J., & Schultz, M. (2010). Toward a theory of brand co-creation with implications for brand governance. *Journal of Brand Management, 17*(8), 590–604.

Heath, R. L. (1992). Critical perspectives on public relations. In E. L. Toth, and R. L. Heath (Eds.), *Rhetorical and critical approaches to public relations*. Thousand Oaks, CA: Sage, pp. 37–61.

Heath, R. L., & Coombs, W. T. (2006). *Today's public relations: An introduction*. Thousand Oaks, CA: Sage.

Jenkins, H. (2006). *Convergence culture: Where old and new media collide*. New York: New York University Press.

Kassing, J. W., & Sanderson, J. (2009). "You're the kind of guy that we all want for a drinking buddy": Expressions of parasocial interaction on floydlandis.com. *Western Journal of Communication, 73*(2), 182–203.

Kassing, J. W., & Sanderson, J. (2010). Fan–athlete interaction and Twitter tweeting through the Giro: A case study. *International journal of sport communication, 3*(1), 113–128.

Keaney, M. (2017). Head of digital media at AS Roma talks about resonating in a connected world. Retrieved from: https://blog.sprinklr.com/as-roma-head-digital-media-paul-rogers/.

Pegoraro, A. (2014). Twitter as disruptive innovation in sport communication. *Communication & Sport, 2*(2), 132–137.

Principles (2019) Retrieved from: https://www.premierleague.com/about/statement-of-principles.

Statement of Mission (2019). Retrieved from: https://www.premierleague.com/about/solidarity.

Sutherland, K., & Barker, R. (2013). Employer expectations of public relations graduates' transmedia storytelling proficiency. *PRism, 10*(1), pp. 1–9.

Sutherland, K., & Barker, R. (2014). The influence of transmedia storytelling portfolio examples on employer perceptions of public relations graduate employability—a pilot study. *Asia Pacific Public Relations Journal, 15*(1), 55–70.

Taylor, M., & Kent, M. L. (2014). Dialogic engagement: Clarifying foundational concepts. *Journal of Public Relations Research, 26*(5), 384–398.

Tenderich, B. (2013). Design elements of transmedia branding. Retrieved from: http://www.edee.gr/files/White_papers_cases_articles/Design%20Elements%20of%20Transmedia%20Branding.pdf.

Van Laer, T., De Ruyter, K., Visconti, L. M., & Wetzels, M. (2014). The extended transportation-imagery model: A meta-analysis of the antecedents and consequences of consumers' narrative transportation. *Journal of Consumer Research, 40*(5), 797–817.

Van Ruler, B. (2015). Agile public relations planning: The reflective communication scrum. *Public Relations Review, 41*(2), 187–194.

Young, P., & Åkerström, M. (2015). Meet the digital naturals. In W. T. Coombs, J. Falkheimer, M. Heide, and P. Young (Eds.), *Strategic communication, social media and democracy: The challenge of the digital naturals.* London: Routledge, pp. 1–10.

10 Culture and Sport

Sport is interwoven and deeply connected with culture. Strategic communicators must appreciate and honor the myriad cultural factors interwoven throughout sport because these factors affect the opportunities and threats found in sport communication. Each of these cultural factors—race, gender, LGBTQ+, (dis)ability, and technology—can affect threats and opportunities. In this chapter, we briefly discuss the ways in which sport has lacked in growth mindset to be inclusive and diverse, and how that lacking results in inequity.

Race and Sport

Two demonstrations might come to mind when thinking about sports activism regarding race: 1) the 1968 Olympics when John Carlos and Tommy Smith raised their black-gloved fists in protest while standing on the Olympic podium to receive their medals; and 2) Colin Kaepernick's #TakeAKnee activism in the NFL. Carlos and Smith raised their fists to demonstrate Black power and support for the human rights movement. Kaepernick and other NFL players took a knee during the playing of the National Anthem at the beginning of NFL games to protest police brutality against Blacks in the U.S. Sport can be a powerful engine in advocacy and provides an international stage for social justice efforts.

Of course, enormous repercussions for the athletes who engage in social justice initiatives can be long-lasting and career-crushing. Still, their work does have a ripple effect. For example, the continued emphasis on social justice matters have since been positioned alongside the Black Lives Matter movement. In 2020, NBA players took a knee during a televised game while wearing Black Lives Matter shirts. LeBron James, after the game told reporters, "We hope we made Kaep proud. We thank him for his efforts." Athletes and their personal brands also are making great strides in their communities and across the nation with generous donations. For example, the Michael Jordan Brand announced a ten-year, $100 million pledge to "organizations dedicated to ensuring racial equality, social justice and greater access to education" (Pitofsky, 2020). In July, a $2.5 million donation was earmarked for

DOI: 10.4324/9781003031161-11

NAACP Legal Defense and Educational Fund, the Formerly Incarcerated, Convicted Peoples and Families Movement and Black Voters Matter.

Race in sport has so many more implications than could be covered if this entire textbook were dedicated solely to the topic. Perhaps among the most important topics remain focused on these acts of social activism by Black athletes and the fight for equity in sport for athletes and staff of color. Racial equity is far from achieved throughout sport. Each year, the Institute for Diversity and Ethics in Sport (TIDES) reports on professional sport organizations' race and gender hiring practices. The report focuses on U.S.-based sports leagues. The 2019 Race and Gender Report named the WNBA and the NBA as industry leaders regarding diverse hiring practices (Lapchick et al., 2019). The NBA is the only men's professional league in the U.S. to score an A rating in hiring people of color. Read sidebar for more details on the 2019 Race and Gender Report.

The 2019 Race and Gender Report from the Institute for Diversity and Ethics in Sport (TIDES) was published in June 2020. The report assigns letter grades to professional and collegiate sports organizations regarding race and gender hiring practices. The grading scale is based upon census demographics. For the 2019 report, to earn an "A" rating for race, 30 percent of an organization's employees need to be people of color; and for gender, 45 percent is needed.

The executive summary for the 2019 Race and Gender Report states (Lapchick et al., 2019):

"Only the Women's National Basketball Association (WNBA) and National Basketball Association (NBA) received an A or better in the overall grade in the 2019 Racial and Gender Report Card. Major League Soccer (MLS) earned a B while Major League Base- ball (MLB) and the National Football League (NFL) earned a B-. College Sport was again the lowest with a C+. While there were no huge shifts in the overall grades, four of the six reports showed a slight decline of between .1 and 2.8 points.

For racial hiring practices, the WNBA and NBA received an A+, MLS got an A, and MLB got an A-. The NFL and college sport received a B. The WNBA, MLS, MLB and college sport increased slightly by between 0.5 and 2.0 points. The NBA stayed the same while the NFL dropped precipitously by 6.7 points. This was the third year in a row where at least four leagues received at least an A- for racial hiring; by contrast five leagues received a C+ or lower for gender hiring.

The gender hiring practices remained more problematic. Only the WNBA received an A. The NBA received a B after four consecu- tive years of declines. Both college sport and the NFL increased their gender scores by 0.7 and 2.0 points, respectively and got a C+ while the MLS and MLB earned a C after dropping by 4.8 and 1.4 points, respectively."

Race and sport is an important and imperative topic that should be at the forefront of any strategic sport communication campaign. From social activism to equity, endless opportunities for improvement exist regarding race in sport.

Gender and Sport

In 1943, a 15-team All-American Girls Professional Baseball League launched as the United States' first professional women's sports league. The league lasted 11 seasons (until 1954) and then it wasn't until 1997 that the Women's National Basketball Association (WNBA) played its first season. In contrast, the NBA was founded in 1946. The National Women's Soccer League (WNSL) was founded in 2012 (the men's league was founded in 1993). The WNBA is the only major league sport to earn a score of "A" regarding gender hiring practices among professional and collegiate sport in the U.S. (Lapchick et al., 2019).

Women play sports, women work in sports, women are sports fans, and women make sports-related purchases. So why are women still a secondary thought regarding all aspects of sport? Title IX is a federal law in the United States established in 1972 to prohibit gender discrimination in high schools and colleges. Title IX asserts that female athletes should be granted equal access to sports opportunities. These opportunities would include access to quality playing fields, uniforms, transportation, and, in some cases, co-ed play. A survey conducted by YouGov in 2019—a full 45 years since the adoption of Title IX—asked respondents how aware they are of Title IX and the protections it offers female athletes. More than half of the respondents answered "not much" or "not at all."

One could argue the same lack of awareness exists among sport apparel manufacturers. Sporting goods stores demonstrate a severe lack in women's sports apparel, especially safety equipment. For example, athletic wear companies make only men's versions of safety equipment for predominately male sports. There are no available football girdles for girls or women to purchase. Girls and women play football but the ill-fitting and mis-gendered safety equipment available for purchase further marginalizes their health and safety on the field. Moreover, WNBA and WNSL jerseys should be sold at large sporting goods chains, just as men's sports team jerseys are, but they are not (Allen, 2020).

Women in sport are gaining ground. Women's sports opportunities are broadening and women are gaining more air time within traditionally male-dominated sports. For example, women have competed in the WWE, or World Wrestling Entertainment, since the 1980s but it was not until the 2000s that WWE women gained momentum in some of the major pay-per-view events. For example, the first women's Royal Rumble match aired in 2018. WWE founder Vince McMahon has passed on to his children much of the business operations. His daughter, Stephanie McMahon Levesque, a WWE superstar and now WWE's chief branding officer, is making great strides in the way the company represents its women athletes. For years, WWE's women wrestlers were coined "Divas" but in 2016 when Levesque became the commissioner of RAW, the championship and accompanying belt was renamed the Women's Championship.

Still, women are sexualized in sport and professional representation of women's sports in media still is grossly lacking. The lack of broadcasted women's sports matches is one area of growth that is often hotly debated. YouGov surveyed American sports fans in 2019 and asked respondents what their level of interest is regarding watching women's sports. Nearly 70 percent of the respondents answered "a little bit" or "not at all interested" compared with 31 percent who answered they are "very interested" or "somewhat interested" in watching women's sports. In fact, 49 percent of sports fans are women themselves and, like all other cultural considerations in sport, representation matters.

In 2010, ESPN started espnW, a blog focused on women's sports. Today, espnW has grown to become one of ESPN's top digital products. ESPN was among the first to dedicate considerable broadcast time to women's sports, but WNBA games, for example, are aired on ESPN2. ABC also broadcasts some WNBA games, and in 2020, the CBS Television Network was set to air its first ever WNBA broadcast—but only one (WNBA.com). The rest were to remain on CBS Sports Network. NBA TV enjoys a partnership with WNBA to broadcast WNBA games. The NBA broadcasting service offers WNBA fans the ability to purchase a WNBA League Pass. Airing WNBA games makes good business sense as WNBA games averaged 413,000 viewers across ESPN2 and ABC—a 64 percent increase year-over-year from 2018's first four games on ESPN2 (Moran, 2019).

Unfortunately, inequities exist in every facet regarding women and sport, not the least of which is the continuous battle regarding unequal pay. In fact, the average salary for men playing in the Premier League is 99 times higher than the top-paid female player (Cox, 2021). As such, the U.S. Women's National Team shook things up in 2020 after winning another World Cup in 2019 when the organization sued the United States Soccer Federation, Inc. regarding unfair pay compared with the U.S. Men's Soccer Team's collective bargaining agreements (Cater, 2020). The lawsuit claimed that the U.S. Soccer Federation violates the Equal Pay Act and Title VII of the Civil Rights Act of 1964. The lawsuit was struck down by federal court but Megan Rapinoe, a USWNT superstar, continues her hard work as an activist for equal pay for women in sport as well as for LGBTQ rights, which is discussed in the next section.

LGBTQ+ and Sport

Lesbian, gay, bisexual, transgender, and queer (LGBTQ) identities in sport remain a controversial topic even though LGBTQ athletes are not at all a new phenomenon. From the battle of homophobia to transgender acceptance, sports are slow to accept this facet of culture. These matters are important to consider and weigh when strategically communicating about sport because a good campaign should not further marginalize already marginalized groups.

Sports reporting and the resultant public discourse regarding athletes publicly "coming out" is repeatedly found by researchers to be initially positive, supportive, and congratulatory in nature yet sports journalists use "coded and overt homophobic labels and language" (Billings et al., 2015; Moscowitz et al., 2019). The reporting and discourse includes conversations regarding the complication and distraction of LGBTQ in sports, and discusses the ways in which athletes are masculine and therefore not stereotypically gay. It is no wonder that is took until 2013 for the first professional male athlete to make a public announcement. Among the first gay male athletes to share their stories were Jason Collins, a center in the National Basketball Association in 2013, and Michael Sam, who was the first collegiate football player to enter the National Football League draft as an openly gay athlete in 2014. Sam never signed with an NFL team and left football altogether in 2015 citing mental health reasons. Since, the battle against homophobia throughout professional sports has raged on and few LGBTQ athletes remain public about their identities.

The decades-long battle against homophobia in sport rages on around the globe—both inside and outside of the locker rooms. Efforts are in full swing to deter discrimination and harassment but sport organizations and leagues still have a long way to go. In the United Kingdom, the first gay men's soccer club was founded in 1991 (Lane, 2021). Stonewall Football Club competes in the Middlesex County League Premier Division and has since won nine International Gay and Lesbian Football Association World Cups. Stonewall FC's mission at inception, and since, has been to "rid the game of football of homophobia." Today. Stonewall FC is among the best playing teams and the players remain active in their collective and individual activism efforts. Stonewall FC also has a second team called "Unity Team." Stonewall's Unity Team "offers an inclusive environment for LGBT+ players of any ability to come and enjoy" the game (Lane, 2021).

In the U.S., among the first orders of business for President Joe Biden was the signing of an executive order that bans discrimination against transgender athletes across all sports. In response to President Biden's executive order, January 2021 ended with a battle of the hashtags: #BidenErasedWomen and #TERFs. The acronym TERF means "trans-exclusionary radical feminist." The online discourse straddled support to vehement phobia in response to the presidential order that now allows transgender women to participate in women's sports leagues (Bowden, 2021). The executive order reads:

> In Bostock v. Clayton County, 590 U.S. ___ (2020), the Supreme Court held that Title VII's prohibition on discrimination "because of … sex" covers discrimination on the basis of gender identity and sexual orientation. Under Bostock's reasoning, laws that prohibit sex discrimination—including Title IX of the Education Amendments of 1972, … the Fair Housing Act, … and section 412 of the Immigration and Nationality

Act, ...—prohibit discrimination on the basis of gender identity or sexual orientation.

The hashtags used online to debate the order expressed how those against allowing transgender women to compete in women's sports claimed there are "biological differences in endurance and muscle mass" that leaves the playing field so uneven that the order "eviscerates women's sports." Those for the executive order cling to the language the president used,

> Every person should be treated with respect and dignity ... be able to learn without worrying about whether they will be denied access to the restroom, the locker room, or school sports ... and be able to earn a living and pursue a vocation knowing that they will not be fired, demoted, or mistreated because of whom they go home to or because how they dress does not conform to sex-based stereotypes.

LGBTQ identities do not define an athlete, their ability, nor their propensity to succeed or fail in their sport. Careful consideration should be extended when communicating about these cultural aspects related to human identity so as to not further limit perceptions. Representation matters in sport and this is one area where strategic sport communication will continue to grow as activism toward equality strengthens.

Sport and Disability

Sport and disability is another important cultural topic when it comes to communicating strategically about sport. Sport is so hyper-focused on ability that disability seems a distant cousin to the overarching topic. This is simply not true. In fact, at the very heart of sport is the overcoming of all personal limitations.

Inclusivity in communicating about sports is imperative. Inclusivity in communication can include written and visual forms. Accessible written communication can include the use of everyday terms and not overcomplicating the written word. Accessibility should also include read-aloud capability or Braille translations. Visual communication is an often overlooked avenue for accessible communication, unfortunately. Color usage should be carefully considered as one in 12 men are colorblind and therefore unable to distinguish between colors, view the brightness of colors, visualize shades of reds and greens, or see any color at all (National Eye Institute). Moreover, blind or visually impaired individuals cannot see or see clearly images, video or other common visual communication elements used in sports media or sport communication. For these reasons, readable alt text that describes what is pictured or shown on the video footage should accompany these visual elements.

From Special Olympics to Paralympics, disability and sport are a celebrated marriage. Special Olympics is an organization that supports lifelong sports activity for children with intellectual disabilities. The organization began in 1968 in the U.S. and has grown to reach around the globe. The website reads: "The transformative power of sports to instill confidence, improve health and inspire a sense of competition is at the core of what Special Olympics does." Both Special Olympics and the Paralympic Games are multi-sports events that include competitors with myriad physical limitations. In the summer and winter Paralympic Games, for example, there are ten allowable disability or types of impairment celebrated through sporting competitions ranging from track and field to skiing, including: "muscle power, impaired passive range of movement, limb deficiency, leg length difference, short stature, hypertonia, ataxia, athetosis, vision impairment and intellectual impairment" (Wikipedia, 2020).

Researchers at Bournemouth conducted a large-scale study to examine the media portrayals of parasports. The researchers note that parasports are watched by more women than men and viewers tend to skew younger as an overall audience. They also pointed out that parasport broadcasts feature female sports and female athletes more often than is shown in traditional sports. Of note, the researchers concluded that parasports viewers expressed they wanted more backstories on the athletes as well as more explanatory details regarding the events and the new/emerging technologies featured in the events (Silk et al., 2019). As media professionals learn to communicate about diverse sport offerings, and grow more inclusive in such coverage, the Bournemouth researchers have this advice:

> There remains a need for further dialogue between broadcasters, disability groups, policy makers, national and international governing bodies with respect to creating opportunity for inclusion and the development of blueprints for broadcasters, and for additional input into how varying forms of impairment are mediated and represented.
>
> (Silk et al., 2019, p. 71)

Some sports leagues are considering fans who are differently abled, too. For example, the Premier League asked its associated teams to consider ways in which they might make their stadiums more accessible. Read Chapter 4's running example regarding sensory rooms offered by the Watford Football Club for fans with autism spectrum disorder (ASD).

Sport and Technology

Technology becomes more integrated into sports with each passing year. Technologies present both opportunities and threats for sport. Here, we discuss how technology has broadened the scope and reach of sports through fan interactivity. The use of second screens, fantasy sports, sports betting, and the explosive growth of eSports across the professional and collegiate levels have all broadened the wide world of sports all across the globe.

Second Screens, Fantasy Sports, and Sports Betting

It is important to consider the many ways in which technology has enhanced sports fans' ability to engage with sports. Second-screen use is one of the most prolific ways in which technology has shaped and reshaped sports consumption, and thus sports marketing. Second-screen use occurs when a person is watching a sporting event on a television screen or is attending a live event and also interacting on other devices across social media platforms. Second-screen use has become so commonplace that brands are working hard across platforms toward brand integration but some research shows evidence that second screens are splintering attention and brand awareness, recall, and recognition suffer as a result (Jensen et al., 2015). One might argue that the pandemic brought on the phenomenon of *third*-screen use where sports fans meet on Zoom on their laptops to "hang out" with friends and fans while watching the sporting event on TV and then tweeting about the experience from their cell phones.

Technology, both hardware and software, affect viewing habits, and viewing habits then determine the battle between subscriptions, pay-per-views, OTT and free-to-air, the increase of all things mobile, and the accompanying marketing and advertising spending on each of these tech platforms and capabilities. Interactivity with technology regarding sport is endless. For example, the new artificial intelligence-powered "virtual concierges" that fans can chat with through online platforms. Satisfi Labs built a bot for the Atlanta Braves that's embedded in the Major League Baseball Ballpark app. This bot answers questions from fans about everything from player stats to the game of baseball in general (Woodford, 2019).

There are countless ways in which technology allows for fans to interact with each other and to better engage with their beloved teams. Technology has allowed for fantasy football leagues to form among friend groups and at large, and technology has allowed for sports betting at a gambler's fingertips, which is not necessarily a good thing. Fan identification and fan behavior can become hyper-invigorated when engaging in these technological advances because fantasy sports or sports betting provides a personal benefit (or loss) beyond team identification. In fact, research has indicated that arousal and self-esteem are heightened over time from interacting with fantasy sports and sports betting (Billings et al., 2017). Given these technologies are relatively new, FanDuel was founded in 2009, DraftKings in 2012, and the Fantasy Sports & Gaming Association just rebranded itself in 2019, growth in activity and spending are occurring at head spinning rates. Moreover, the reason these two interactive sport technologies—fantasy sports and sports betting—are grouped together is because the users of these technologies are so similar (Fantasy Sports & Gaming Association, 2019). In fact, in the 2019 survey conducted by the Fantasy Sports & Gaming Association, user demographics are nearly identical. See Box 10.1 for details.

BOX 10.1 Fantasy and betting demographics

Demographics:

Fantasy players

81% male, 19% female
50% are between the ages of 18–34 (average age is 37.7)
67% are employed full-time
47% make more than $75,000 (national average is 34%)

Sports bettors

80% male, 20% female
50% are between the ages of 18–34 (average age is 38.1)
67% are employed full-time
45% make more than $75,000 (national average is 34%)

Collective crossover: 78% of fantasy sports players bet on sports in 2018. And 75% of sports bettors played fantasy sports in 2018 (Fantasy Sports & Gaming Association, 2019).

Fantasy players, which have grown to include 45.9 million players, and sports bettors are most likely to engage with American football than any other sport. At the least percentage, just over 5 million fantasy players, or 11 percent, interact with eSports. eSports in gaining favor among sports bettors, too, as 15 percent actively place wagers on these video-game matches.

eSports

The eSports phenomenon has quickly spread around the world, intriguing sports fans and video-game players, packing large stadiums around the globe, all while being live-streamed by mainstream sports media outlets complete with sports reporters' commentary. eSports is now deemed its own sport at both the professional and collegiate levels with players vying for the winning title as they perform in virtual worlds in front of tens of thousands of fans at live events or live streams. At the collegiate level, eSports programs and varsity teams are popping up on campuses across the U.S. For example, the University of Kentucky has launched an active eSports program, and shares content across numerous media platforms: YouTube, Twitch, Twitter, and Discord, just to name a few. Collegiate conferences have formed, including the National Association of Collegiate eSports (NACE), which had 175 member schools enrolled in 2019. NACE hosts varsity-level eSports competitions and summer combines, and academic scholarships are becoming widely available for varsity eSports players. To put this into perspective, varsity collegiate sports generally require multiple millions of dollars to support the program and to be competitive, especially at the D-1 level. The fact that universities are launching varsity eSports fresh from the launch of the program is a startling contrast to the decades-long club sports existence for sports like lacrosse.

On the professional side of eSports, revenue reached $1 billion in 2020 and activity in the sport and attendance of events has doubled each year since 2015 with an estimated 250 million viewers in 2019, according to the eSports Trade Association. eSports is also big on brand sponsorships, having totaled $897 million in 2019, and eSports partners with nonprofit and for profit businesses around the globe. This is one area that COVID-19 did not cripple activity in sport. ESPN eSports features journalist commentators during the matches. Sponsorships and ad placements are available for purchase, and the deals include [bot]chat mentions periodically complete with a live link to the product or service advertised.

This chapter has reviewed the endless ways in which sport and culture collide. From identity to tech and inequity to representation, there is so much work to be accomplished across global strategic sport communication campaigns. The biggest question remains where to begin.

References

Allen, S. (2020, August 26). An 11-year-old girl went in search of her favorite WNBA star's shoes. She found her voice instead. *The Washington Post*. Retrieved from https://www.chron.com/lifestyle/article/An-11-year-old-girl-went-in-search-of-her-15517421.php

Billings, A. C., Moscowitz, L. M., Rae, C., & Brown-Devlin, N. (2015). The art of coming out: Traditional and social media frames surrounding the NBA's Jason Collins. *Journalism & Mass Communication Quarterly*, *92*(1), 142–160.

Billings, A., Ruihley, B. J., & Yang, Y. (2017). Fantasy gaming on steroids? Contrasting fantasy sport participation by daily fantasy sport participation. *Communication & Sport*, *5*(6), 732–750.

Bowden, E. (2021, January 21). Biden sparks TERF war with gender discrimination order. *NYPost.com*. Available online at https://nypost.com/2021/01/21/joe-biden-sparks-terf-war-with-gender-discrimination-order/.

Cater, F. (2020, May 2). Federal Judge Dismisses U.S. Women's Soccer Team's Equal Pay Claim. *NPR*. Available online at https://www.npr.org/2020/05/02/849492863/federal-judge-dismisses-u-s-womens-soccer-team-s-equal-pay-claim.

Cox, J. (2021, February 22). Illusory level playing fields: The off-pitch battles facing women's soccer. Forbes. Available online at https://www.forbes.com/sites/josiecox/2021/02/22/illusory-level-playing-fields-the-off-pitch-battles-facing-womens-soccer/?sh=6c8e830d37e5.

ETSA (2020, July 10). Toyota focuses on eSports to boost fan base as motorsport shuts down. Available online at https://esportsta.org/2020/07/toyota-focuses-on-esports-to-boost-fan-base-as-motorsport-shuts-down/

Executive Order on Preventing and Combating Discrimination on the Basis of Gender Identity or Sexual Orientation (2021, January 21). White House,

Presidential Actions. Available online at https://www.whitehouse.gov/briefing-room/presidential-actions/2021/01/20/executive-order-preventing-and-combating-discrimination-on-basis-of-gender-identity-or-sexual-orientation/.

Fantasy Sports & Gaming Association (2019). Industry demographics. Available online at https://thefsga.org/industry-demographics/.

Jensen, J. A., Walsh, P., Cobbs, J., & Turner, B. A. (2015). The effects of second screen use on sponsor brand awareness: A dual coding theory perspective. *Journal of Consumer Marketing*, *32*(2), 71–84.

Lane, B. (2021, January 15). 'The founding mission is not to exist': Stonewall FC, a pioneering LGBT+ soccer team has changed the sport for gay men, now it's pushing to eradicate homophobia in football. *Insider*. Available online at https://www.insider.com/stonewall-fc-pioneering-lgbt-soccer-team-pushes-end-football-homophobia-2021-1.

Lapchick, R. E., Ellis, C., ... & Zimmerman, D. (2019). Racial and Gender Report Card. TIDES. Available online at https://43530132-36e9-4f52-811a-182c7a91933b.filesusr.com/ugd/7d86e5_517e71c07bdc45e4b9a5c053dcbe3108.pdf.

Moran, E. (August 2, 2019). First half viewership spike has WNBA optimistic about 2019 and beyond. Accessed online at https://frntofficesport.com/wnba-viewership-growth/

Moscowitz, L. M., Billings, A. C., Ejaz, K., & O'Boyle, J. (2019). Outside the sports closet: News discourses of professional gay male athletes in the mainstream. *Journal of Communication Inquiry*, *43*(3), 249–271.

National Eye Institute. Color Blindness. Accessed online at https://www.nei.nih.gov/learn-about-eye-health/eye-conditions-and-diseases/color-blindness.

Pitofsky, M. (2020, July 30). Michael Jordan donates $2.5 million to combat voter suppression. *The Hill*. Accessed at https://thehill.com/blogs/in-the-know/in-the-know/509850-michal-jordan-donates-25-million-to-combat-voter-suppression

Silk, M., Pullen, E., Jackson, D., Rich, E., Misener, L., Howe, D., ... & Stutterheim, K. (2019). Re-presenting para-sport bodies: Disability and the cultural legacy of the Paralympic Games. Available online at http://eprints.bournemouth.ac.uk/33236/.

Special Olympics. History, Our Mission. Accessed online at https://www.specialolympics.org/about/history

Wikipedia. (2020, October 30) Paralympic Games. Accessed online at https://en.wikipedia.org/wiki/Paralympic_Games.

WNBA (2020). 2020 WNBA National TV Schedule. Available online at https://www.wnba.com/national-tv-schedule/

Woodford, N. (2019, May 13). Sports advertising and the future of media. *Unruly*. Available online at https://unruly.co/blog/article/2019/05/13/sports-advertising-future/

11 Athlete Health and Safety

Concern over athlete health may seem like a no-brainer but keeping athletes healthy and safe is imperative to all business operations in sport. Athletes face serious risks in sport and global sporting organizations still do not have full-proof solutions for protecting athletes from every harm. In this chapter, we will discuss some of the more prevalent athlete health and safety concerns, as well as the operational and reputational threats that come with each of these athlete health and safety concerns.

Athlete Health and Safety

Sport is intricately linked with health and yet from taped knees to scuffed helmets, athlete bodies are war-tattered from their sport. Some health and safety experts even akin a professional athlete's physical toll from game matchups to being in an automobile crash each week. Sports injuries, from minor to severe, and chronic pain are everyday obstacles for athletes to face and overcome.

It is important to keep in mind that athlete health and safety transcends any one sport organization. And each sport has its own set of concerns that emerge regarding player health and safety. In this chapter, we review sports-related concussions as a major athlete health and safety factor in football, soccer, boxing, and mixed martial arts; and explain why doping holds world-wide health and safety implications across all sports. These health concerns, along with the many more unnamed in this chapter, are threats to sport organizations. Each demonstrate the myriad historical operational threats as well. Still, where threats exists, so too does opportunity.

Concussions: Chronic Traumatic Encephalopathy (CTE)

Perhaps the health and safety issue of most concern is that of traumatic brain injuries. Sports are combative and dangerous to the human body in countless ways but few injuries are more serious or longer-lasting than the concussion crisis in sport. Concussions lead to chronic traumatic encephalopathy (CTE). CTE is a degenerative brain disease that is caused by repeated trauma to the brain.

DOI: 10.4324/9781003031161-12

Concussions, or any other form of mild or severe traumatic brain injury (TBI), are common in sport but the number of concussions endured by players are higher in prevalence in some sports. One study conducted at the CTE Center at Boston University examined 202 brains of football players. Among those brains were 111 that belonged to athletes who competed on the NFL gridiron. All but one of those NFL athletes' brains demonstrated signs of CTE—that's 110 brains with CTE out 111 brains. This particular study found the highest prevalence of CTE among football players in the linemen position.

The Boston study revealed that the brains of NFL linemen are especially at risk because, each time trauma occurs to the head (think of the helmet and pads crashing sound heard when the ball is snapped at the beginning of every play), the brain is jarred and that damage and the brain's response to that damage continues across an athlete's life span—from little league through the pros. In fact, CTE symptoms—which include memory loss, confusion, impaired judgment, impulse control problems, aggression, depression, anxiety, suicidality, parkinsonism, and, eventually, progressive dementia—often do not begin until years after the last brain trauma or end of active athletic involvement (Boston University CTE Research Center).

Prevalence of CTE is not limited to American football. In fact, studies show that hand-to-hand combat sports like boxing, mixed martial arts, and wrestling have just as high a prevalence rate as football. This is true regarding soccer and hockey, as well.

The research, communication, and public health campaigns regarding CTE has brought on a long-term reputational crisis for American football, in particular. Participation in youth leagues has drastically declined over the past decade. In fact, school districts across the country must combine schools to make a full football team to compete each season.

The threats to sport organizations are widespread. First and foremost the deterioration of any athlete's health and wellbeing is a tragic loss for the individual and their family. The healthcare costs for chronic degenerative disease are astronomical. The societal costs also are too great to fully realize. At the organizational level, financial and reputational crises occur. For example, in 2012, over 4,500 NFL players brought a costly and lengthy class action legal suit against the NFL for the CTE prevalence among its players. Almost a decade has past and the class action suit is still being litigated

"Doping": Performance-Enhancing Drugs (PEDs)

Doping is another health and safety issue in sport. Doping is an ideographic term used to encapsulate all forms of performance-enhancing drugs (PEDs) used by athletes. PEDs are used to enhance performance, increase endurance, and make the user stronger, faster, and more capable. PEDs include anything from steroids, to human growth hormone to testosterone to blood transfusions. PEDs are believed to provide a competitive edge. In reality, however, any type of PED use, or doping, has serious health and safety consequences. Doping can even be fatal—to both health and to reputation.

Doping is typically viewed as cheating in professional and collegiate sports. Athletes, sports teams and leagues, and even countries are alleged serial offenders. Examples include a series of incidences throughout the 2000s involving cyclists Lance Armstrong and Floyd Landis, several Major League Baseball players including Roger Clemens, Barry Bonds, Mark McGwire, and Sammy Sosa. Doping also occurs at the collegiate level, like when the National Collegiate Athletic Association (NCAA) sanctioned Syracuse University's men's basketball team in 2015. At the country and Olympics levels, the Russian Olympic track and field team was barred from competing in the 2016 Rio Olympics over its government-sanctioned PED use. In total, Russia allegedly had up to 200 athletes who were caught doping and competing. As a result, Russia was stripped of 47 Olympic medals.

To address this worldwide problem in sports, the World Anti-Doping Agency (WADA) was created in 1999 to govern global oversight of doping in sport. The creation of WADA was in response to, among other things, the Tour de France cyclists' use of PEDs. WADA focuses on four specific facets of oversight: 1) code creation and compliance; 2) research and medicine oversight of doping substances and methods; 3) laboratory accreditation and management; and 4) cooperation with law and governmental officials (WADA, 2015).

The problem with doping, aside from its serious consequences to athlete health and safety and being earmarked as a form of cheating, is that doping is hard to prove without conducting years-long expensive laboratory testing. As such, denial is a common response to accusations of doping. Athletes have historically been advised to deny doping accusations and because of the lengthy and costly endeavor it would be to prove otherwise, this is a successful strategy. However, denial causes distrust among stakeholders. See Box 11.1 for a case of athlete denial for doping.

BOX 11.1 Denial and performance-enhancing drugs: the Marion Jones case

Marion Jones was one of the track and field stars of the 2000 Olympic Games in Sydney, Australia. She won three gold medals (100M, 200M, and 4 x 400M relay) and two bronze medals (long jump and 4 x 100M relay). Jones's success translated into multi-million dollar endorsement deals. In 2004, she was accused of taking performance-enhancing drugs from Victor Conte, head of the Bay Area Laboratory Co-operative (BALCO). BALCO was involved in a number of high-profile performance-enhancing drug cases. Jones immediately denied all charges. The denial was the favored option as she fought the test results and tried to protect her endorsement money. In 2007, Jones acknowledged taking performance-enhancing drugs prior to the 2000 Olympics. As a result of the violation, Jones was stripped of all Olympic medals, lost her endorsement deals, and was sentenced to prison time for lying to authorities about her involvement with BALCO (Associated Press, 2007). The Marion Jones case illustrates how and why athletes will use the denial response during a performance-enhancing drug crisis. Denial is the best option if the athlete hopes to retain sponsors and remain competitive (Coombs, 2018). Of course denial only works if the authorities fail to prove the use of performance-enhancing drugs.

COVID-19 Pandemic

No discussion on athlete health and safety could be complete now without at least a brief nod regarding the handling of athlete health and safety during the COVID-19 global pandemic. The pandemic brought to life the many complicated facets regarding the balancing of athlete health and safety with "the show must go on" financial and operational needs of sport organizations. At the global, professional, and collegiate levels of play, athletes underwent census testing and tracing, and quarantine often was prescribed for teammates of athletes who tested positive. Matches were played without fans present and the COVID-19 global pandemic cost all sport organizations and collegiate athletic departments billions of dollars in lost income.

Professional Athlete Health and Safety during the COVID-19 Pandemic

Pandemic responses across sports leagues varied by the countries in which those leagues operated. The political and social responses to the pandemic were mirrored or even at times at odds with another. For example, the English Premier League continued to play while the NBA abruptly ceased games on March 11, 2020.

By July, the "NBA bubble" began formation as players, staff, and even select members of sports media all reported to the ESPN Wide World of Sports Complex at the Walt Disney World Resort in Orlando, Florida. After weeks of seclusion from family, friends, and the general public, NBA players began playing a series of seeding games before they finally were able to host the league's playoffs from the season that began the year prior. The NBA bubble was not without its challenges. Serious concerns regarding athlete mental health were discussed, and the bubble did not prove impervious to coronavirus. The WNBA also chose the bubble route. The "Wubble" was hosted at the IMG Academy in Bradenton, Florida and did prove impervious to a coronavirus outbreak. The WNBA enjoyed a successful season, albeit without fans in the stands just like all other 2020 major league sports in America—until the NFL's Super Bowl in Florida was hosted in February 2021. The NBA bubble cost the league $180 million. That sounds like a lot until you realize the bubble saved the league from losing $1.5 in revenue from sponsorship deals and broadcast contracts. Of course, all revenue from ticket sales during the bubble were lost but the NBA maintained its other revenue sources (Beer, 2020).

Collegiate Athlete Health and Safety during the COVID-19 Pandemic

In the U.S., divergent rules were applied to university students and student athletes, especially at the large power conference schools where collegiate athletics are multimillion dollar operations.

Student athletes continued to practice while the general student population were sent home or asked to stay home and attend online courses. Universities throughout the United States oftentimes followed county or state school closing and reopening guidelines, and based athletic competition decisions upon those guidelines, making the playing field uneven within and across conferences. In total, 139 NCAA football games were either canceled or postponed due to COVID-19 (Cobb, Kercheval, & Sallee, 2020). Two of college football's power five conferences halted play altogether: the Big 10 and the PAC 12. The Big 10 announced that five of its Covid-positive athletes contracted myocarditis and the conference did want to put more players at risk (Nocera, 2020). All five conferences ended up playing in some capacity as the fall semester limped along in 2020. Games were regularly cancelled or rescheduled. In fact, 19.7 percent of regular season games were cancelled and so were 39 percent of the bowl games (Forde & Dellengerjan, 2021). Still, conference revenue remained mostly steady for FY2020 because most payouts were situated prior to the COVID-19 season halts, however, drastic cuts to payouts the tune of at least $12M are expected for FY2021 (Wilner, 2021).

Some student athletes felt pressured to play to keep their scholarships or to realize their dream to one day play in the pros. Demands to play and requests for health equity emerged amongst collegiate athletes as they protested on social media with the hashtag, #WeWantToPlay. Athletes from all five of the power college conferences tweeted #WeAreUnited with a set of proposed rules and best practices they wished for all conferences to adopt so athletes could choose whether to play and so they could play safely. Their requests included universal mandated procedures and protocols, a protected opt-out option, guaranteed eligibility whether the athlete chooses to play or not, and a safe season of play.

Student athletes also were concerned about their health and wellbeing, especially regarding the reports that were emerging that coronavirus could weaken or inflame the heart muscle of collegiate athletes. Physicians at Ohio State University found myocarditis in four of the 26 college athletes they tested, post COVID-positive, and researchers at West Virginia University "examined 54 student athletes who had tested positive for COVID-19 three to five weeks earlier" and found "a lot of evidence of pericarditis" (Sengupta, 2020). Nearly half of the WVU athletes had inflammation around the heart and more than half of them had excess fluid around the heart.

The actions of the colleges and universities also affected community health. Peaks in positive cases rose in communities when classes resumed at local universities. Some universities, such as the University of Alabama and The University of North Carolina at Chapel Hill faced crisis situations over students celebrating game outcomes en masse, and thus allegedly putting the surrounding communities at risk. In addition, simply playing games with limited fans increased the spread of the virus. Data collected after Texas A&M University home football games showed a spike in COVID-19 within ten days of that home game (Witte, 2020).

The pandemic limited some athletes' ability to workouts in gyms or training at the same capacity as prior to the pandemic. It will be years before the true lasting impact of the pandemic will be known regarding the physical and mental health of collegiate and professional athletes.

Athlete Health and Safety: Technology

From mouthguards to AstroTurf to sensor-embedded clothing, athlete health and safety is ever-evolving with technological advancements. Even the battle against heat exhaustion is being won with the evolutionary improvements of wearable sensors that calculate and then help to calibrate body temperature with wearable cooling systems athletes can utilize when competing in extreme weather conditions (Muniz-Pardos et al., 2019). Athletes often compete in extreme weather conditions. Heat, in particular, is of special concern due to exertional heat illness that can result from increased core temperatures caused by physical exhertion. Heat illness can impair coordination, cognitive function, and endurance performance, and can result in heat stroke, which is life-threatening. Research indicates that survival is greatly increased when interventions are delivered within 30 minutes of a heat stroke. Wearable sensors and cooling systems are of particular importance during summer Olympics competitions where athletes have experienced exertional heat illness resulting in 104+ degree body temperatures during competition in such hot and humid host cities as Los Angeles (1984), Athens (2004), Beijing (2008), and Rio de Janeiro (2016).

Efforts to reduce sports-related concussions are springing up through concussive impact detection devices and the use of the head impact telemetry (HIT) systems in helmets. The National Football League (NFL) and Amazon Web Services (AWS) announced a partnership to develop a computer simulation model that replicates on-field scenarios called the Digital Athlete. The Digital Athlete is an AI, machine learning, and computer vision technology that is being used to identify ways in which the league can reduce, treat, and rehabilitate sports-related injuries (NFL, 2019). One way the Digital Athlete has aided NFL athletes was with preliminary data indicating an increased chance for concussions on game kick-offs. The league implemented a new kick-off rule in 2018 as a result and a 38 percent decrease in concussions on game kick-offs have resulted from that rule change.

Conclusion

The health and safety of athletes should never be compromised and should always remain top-of-mind. The head-in-the-sand approach to athlete health and safety is outdated and no longer an acceptable approach. Sport organizations should regularly conduct risk–benefit analyses of current operational practices and any risks to athlete health and safety that might be present within those operations. Leagues and advocacy groups are working together on rule changes and equipment enhancements to protect players, and as technology continues to develop, sport organizations can continue to explore the many ways in which sports can become safer for all.

References

Associated Press (2007). Legal issues have left Marion Jones nearly broke. Retrieved from Legal issues have left Marion Jones nearly broke (espn.com)

Beer, T. (2020). Perot: NBA's bubble prevented $1.5 billion in losses. Retrieved from Report: NBA's Bubble Prevented $1.5 Billion In Losses (forbes.com)

Boston University Research: CTE Center. Frequently asked questions about CTE. Accessed online at https://www.bu.edu/cte/about/frequently-asked-questions/

Cobb, D., Kercheval, B., & U Sallee, B. (2020). College football sees 139 games canceled or postponed during the 2020 regular season due to COVID-19 issues. Retrieved from College football sees 139 games canceled or postponed during 2020 regular season due to COVID-19 issues – CBSSports.com.

Coombs, W. T. (2018). Athlete reputational crises: One point for linking situational crisis communication theory and sports crises. In A.C. Billings, W.T. Coombs, & K.A. Brown (eds.) *Reputational challenges in sport: Theory and application* (pp. 13–24). New York: Routledge.

Forde, P., & Dellengerjan, R. (2021, January 11). Was the 2020 college football season worth it? *Sports Illustrated.* Available online at https://www.si.com/college/2021/01/11/college-football-2020-season-covid-19-daily-cover.

Muniz-Pardos, B., Sutehall, S., Angeloudis, K., Shurlock, J., & Pitsiladis, Y. P. (2019). The use of technology to protect the health of athletes during sporting competitions in the heat. *Frontiers in Sports and Active Living, 1,* 38. https://doi.org/10.3389/fspor.2019.00038

NFL (2019, December 5) Using artificial intelligence to advance player health and safety. https://www.nfl.com/playerhealthandsafety/equipment-and-innovation/aws-partnership/using-artificial-intelligence-to-advance-player-health-and-safety

Nocera, J. (2020, November 13). College football in covid time is a failure. Surprised? *Bloomberg Business.* Available online at https://www.bloomberg.com/opinion/articles/2020-11-13/big-10-and-pac-12-college-football-during-covid-is-a-failure.

Sengupta, P. (2020, November 4). Even if you're asymptomatic, COVID-19 can harm your heart, study shows – here's what student athletes need to know. *The Conversation.* Accessed online at https://theconversation.com/even-if-youre-asymptomatic-covid-19-can-harm-your-heart-study-shows-heres-what-student-athletes-need-to-know-149243.

Topolosky, A. (2020, August 18). One bat mitzvah girl's slam dunk story. *The New York Jewish Week.* Acessed online at https://jewishweek.timesofisrael.com/one-bat-mitzvah-girls-slam-dunk-story/

Ward, J., Williams, J., & Manchester, S. (2017, July 25). 110 NFL Brains. *New York Times*. Accessed online at https://www.nytimes.com/interactive/2017/07/25/sports/football/nfl-cte.html

WADA (2015). Independent Commission Report: Background on WADA, Terms of Reference. [Online] Retrieved from https://www.wada-ama.org/en/resources/independent-commission-terms-of-reference.

Wilner, J. (2021, January 29). Pac-12 financial documents: Conference met its obligations, dodged a COVID cash crunch in FY20. Available online at https://www.mercurynews.com/2021/01/29/pac-12-financial-documents-conference-met-its-obligations-dodged-a-covid-cash-crunch-in-fy20/.

Witte, K. (2020). COVID in context: Tracking the spike two weeks after Kyle Field reopened to fans. Retrieved from COVID in Context: Tracking the spike two weeks after Kyle Field reopened to fans (kbtx.com)

12 Crisis Communication and Reputation Management in Sports

Throughout this book we have emphasized how strategic communication should contribute to the success of an organization. Revenue is the obvious measure of success. A profit-making sports organization needs to generate more revenue than it expends. In addition to revenue, reputation is a highly valued asset for all organizations. Reputation is a form of social evaluation and represents how people feel about the organization. Managers worry about reputations because a strong, favorable reputation makes an organization more attractive to customers, employees, and investors (Davies, Chun, da Silva, & Roper, 2003). The NBA's falling out with China in 2019 is an example of how reputation and revenue are interconnected. Comments in support of Hong Kong protestors by one NBA employee cost NBA around $400 million. Crises are threats to an organization's reputation (Barton, 2001). Crisis management is the larger strategic process designed to lessen the negative effects from a crisis including reputational damage (Bundy, Pfarrer, Short, & Coombs, 2017). Strategic communication can be invaluable during a crisis because crisis communication can lessen reputation damage when done properly or can make the crisis worse when done improperly. Crisis communication is the lifeblood of crisis management—it brings crisis management to life. The focus on this chapter is to provide the essential background knowledge for crisis managers, to identify what makes for effective and ineffective crisis communication, and to note the unique context sports creates for crisis communication.

Basics of Crisis Management

The term crisis is often used as a label for any negative situation. In an organization, it is a mistake to think of a bad day or a minor problem as a crisis. Crisis is reserved for the big problems. Using the term crisis means there is a serious threat facing the organization that demands the full attention of management. We can define a crisis as "the perceived violation of salient stakeholder expectations that can create negative outcomes for stakeholders and/or the organization" (Coombs, 2019, p. 3). Crises are perceptual. If people think everything fine, there is no crisis. When stakeholders

DOI: 10.4324/9781003031161-13

think there is a violation of salient expectations, there is a crisis. Salient expectations are important to stakeholders, they matter. Examples of salient expectations include safety of products, quality of products, behavior of employees, treatment of workers, respect for the environment, and responsible sourcing of raw materials. The negative outcomes from a crisis can affect stakeholders and/or the organization. Stakeholders can be placed at risk by a harmful product or be angered when an organization sources raw material from an irresponsible supplier. Organizations can suffer a drop in sales, loss of market share, a decline in stock price, and/or damage to organizational reputation from a crisis. Crisis communication seeks to lessen the negative outcomes for both the stakeholders affected by the crisis and the organization in crisis.

We tend to think of a crisis as an event, something that happens or someone does something. A player is found to have used a performance-enhancing drug or a bomb explodes near the team's bus that is filled with players. But sometimes a crisis is a realization that stakeholders now see the organization in a negative light. It is not an event but rather a shift in societal values that now define once acceptable practices as a problem. The Washington Football Team ended the use of its racist name ("Redskins") only after a seismic shift in most of the U.S. public developed a greater sensitivity to racial concerns in 2020. The reputational damage from keeping the name had finally outweighed the case for keeping the name. Various groups had complained about the team name for years but it was the shift in societal values that created the crisis for the Washington Football Team.

It is helpful for crisis managers to think of a crisis as a process. By treating a crisis as a process, crisis managers can see how the crisis management and communication is a serious of actions and not just the public response to the crisis. It is common to think of crisis as a three-phased process: 1) pre-crisis, 2) crisis response, and 3) post-crisis. Pre-crisis includes efforts to mitigate against a crisis occurring and preparing to respond to a crisis. The crisis response represents what an organization says and does after the crisis emerges. Post-crisis are actions taken as the crisis is winding down and include providing update information, mourning (when necessary), and learning from the crisis (Coombs, 2019). The next section will explore each of these phases in more detail.

You might be thinking, "Some of this does not apply to sports." You would be right. Sports teams, for instance, do not make products that could harm consumers such as vehicles with bad brakes. In fact, sports crises are much more likely to threaten the organization than its stakeholders. Moreover, sports crises tend to create reputational damage to the organization rather than operational disruptions (Koerber & Zabara, 2017). However, sports organization are not immune from operational disruptions. COVID-19 was an operational disruption for sport globally. Sports could not be delivered resulting in massive revenue loss. In European football, disruptive fan behavior has caused games to be paused or cancelled. When crises disrupt operations, organizations lose money in addition to suffering reputational damage. Keep in mind that reputational damage does translate into revenue loss as well. Crises in sports tend to have a much stronger reputational focus than crises in other types of organizations (Coombs, 2018).

The connections between reputation and sports is so strong, researchers have identified athlete reputational crisis (ARC) as a distinct form of crisis found in sport. An ARC is "an event caused by (un)intentional and on (off) field athlete behaviors that threaten to disrupt an athlete's reputation" (Sato, Ko, Park, & Tao, 2015, p. 435). There are four types of arcs that reflect if the behavior was intentional or unintentional and on the field or off the field. Box 12.1 provides more details and examples of the four ARCs. The focus is on the athletes and what they do. But other people in an organization can trigger a crisis. It was a general manager's comments that created the China crisis for the NBA. Furthermore, the crisis may be more of a team or league problem. When NFL players questioned if it was safe to go to training camp and play during a pandemic, that was a league crisis for the NFL created by the league's lack of action on safety issues. ARCs are just one example of how crisis communication is unique with in the sports context. In other organizations, an employee misbehaving will not attract the media attention and have the potential to be a crisis as with players. If a worker at a food production facility gets a DUI, the media do not care and there is no crisis. Now a CEO is a different matter. But if a player gets a DUI, that is an ARC.

BOX 12.1 Athlete reputational crises

1. Intentional and on the field: a purposeful action designed to affect athletic performance

    •   Example: Knowingly taking performance-enhancing drugs

2. Unintentional and on the field: an athlete does something that unknowingly affects athletic performance

    •   Example: Taking a cold medication not knowing an ingredient was on the banned list

3. Intentional and off the field: a purposeful action that non-performance related but is viewed as inappropriate or wrong

    •   Example: A player engages in domestic violence

4. Unintentional and off the field: a player accidently does something wrong or inappropriate

    •   Example: A player crashes a vehicle late at night and leaves the scene of the accident

---

BOX 12.2 Scansis and crisis communication

All crises are negative but some are more difficult to manage than others. The Crisis Communication Think Tank at the University of Georgia refers to these extremely difficult crises as sticky crises (Coombs, Holladay, & White, 2021). Sticky crises are more complicated and problematic than your "average" crisis. One type of sticky crisis that you may encounter in sports is the scansis. The scansis is when a crisis is also a scandal. Scandals have a moral component that involve some violation of a moral code/unethical behavior. A scansis is unique because it evokes moral outrage from stakeholders (Coombs & Tachkova, 2019). Moral outrage is a unique, negative emotion that occurs when people perceive a situation was caused by a combination of injustice and greed. The injustice means people were wronged in some way while greed is the motivation for the injustice (Antonetti & Maklan, 2016). A scansis will emerge when people believe someone acted purposeful in a way that was unjust to others for financial gain (greed). Many ARCs can be scanses. An athlete purposefully takes a performance enhancing drug to create an unfair competitive advantage (injustice) and do so to increase his or her own revenue (greed).

The moral outrage is what makes a scansis a sticky crisis and difficult to manage. The typical use of the ethical base response combined with an apology and/or compensation does little to improve how people feel a scansis. Instead, the crisis manager must specifically state the moral violation that has been committed (show an understanding that they know what they did was wrong) and what steps they are taking to prevent a repeat of that action (Coombs & Tachkova, 2019).

Damaged reputations can be a serious concern for organizations, especially when the crisis becomes a scansis, a crisis that is also a scandal. A scansis raises moral concerns and creates a very challenging crisis to manage. Box 12.2 provides additional details about the scansis crisis.

Crisis Communication and the Crisis Lifecycle

Now let us return to the three crisis phases and explore the role of crisis communication at each phase in greater depth. This section will talk in general about crisis communication during the three phases. Later, we will consider specific applications in the sport context.

Pre-Crisis

The pre-crisis phase is about mitigation and preparation. Organizations are constantly in the pre-crisis phase. Mitigation are efforts to prevent a risk from becoming a crisis. Risks have the potential to do harm and a crisis occurs when the risk becomes manifest (Heath, 2010). Mitigation means you take actions you hope will reduce the likelihood of a risk manifesting into a crisis. To mitigate, you first need to find the possible risks. Strategic communicators already know to scan the environment for threats and opportunities. We focus on the threat part when trying to identify risks. Social listening is an excellent example of how strategic communicators can help to locate risks that might need mitigation. A sudden shift in sentiment from positive to negative is a risk signal. Crisis managers try to collect all possible risk information to locate those risks that require mitigation attempts. This broad view of understanding risk is called enterprise risk management (ERM).

The emergence of risk on social media has helped give rise to the paracrisis. A paracrisis is when an organization has to manage a risk in public view. Your stakeholders can see what you are doing or failing to do to manage a risk. The earlier example of the NFL players questioning safety was a paracrisis not a true crisis. Paracrises look like crises but are not as serious (but could become serious) and crisis managers have a wider range of communication options than in a crisis (Coombs & Holladay, 2012). For example, you might ignore a paracrisis because the risk is minimal but you cannot ignore a true crisis and expect a favorable outcome. Box 12.3 provides some additional information about paracrises and communication options.

BOX 12.3 Paracrises and responses

Types of Paracrises

1. Challenge: stakeholders claim that existing organizational practices are irresponsible.
2. Faux Pas: the organization takes an action thinking it will be good (has good intentions) but stakeholders view the action as negative.
3. Social Media Misuse: organization violates the rules for using a social media platform.
4. Guilt by Association: some negatively viewed actor is linked to the organization.
5. Misinformation: unverified and negative information circulates about an organization.
6. Social Media Account Hacking: an organization's social media account is hacked and misused.

Paracrisis Response Strategies

1. Refusal: the organization ignores the paracrisis.
2. Refutation: the organization denies it is wrong.
3. Repression: the organization seeks to silence those criticizing the organization.

4. Recognition: the organization acknowledges there is a problem but takes no action.
5. Revision: the organization takes action to change what stakeholders claim is wrong.
6. Reference to Organizational Values: organization refers to its values and their continued commitment to those values.
7. Dissociation: separate the organization from the source that generates the negativity (Chen, 2019).

Not all mitigation efforts work nor will you be able to catch all risks before they become crises. That is why crisis managers need to invest in preparation. The crisis communication for preparation involves creating the crisis communication plan (CCP) and training the crisis team. The CCP saves time, money, and perhaps lives during a crisis. The CCP is *not* a specific list of steps to management a crisis. Rather, the CCP pre-drafts certain crisis messages, pre-assigns crisis tasks, identifies contact information, and collects the information the crisis team might need during specific crisis situations. By predicting the mostly likely crises you will encounter, a crisis manager can pre-draft basic messages and fill in the details with the crisis hits. A team, for example, knows a player might use performance-enhancing drugs or face legal charges and can pre-draft messages for those crises that are also pre-approved by legal. The pre-drafted messages allow the organization to response fast with its initial message, often called a holding statement. You are holding until you get more information to report. By pre-assigning tasks, the crisis teams know what to do when a crisis hits. Time is saved because you do not have to decide who will do what. Contact information makes it easier to reach experts you might need to help with your crisis. Finally, the crisis manager can collect relevant information for various crises. This is not part of the CCP; you want to keep that document short. The additional information you might need is placed in a separate crisis appendix (Coombs, 2019).

The crisis team is composed of the members of the organization tasked with managing the crisis. Various people can be on a crisis team and the exact composition can vary according to the crisis. Was your team's web site hacked? You will need the technology people on the crisis team. If the crisis involves domestic violence, no need for the technology people. Strategic communication and legal are the two areas you always want on the crisis team (Coombs, 2019). People no not naturally know how to work in teams or manage a crisis. The crisis team needs to practice working as a team and handling various crisis situations. Crisis teams need to train at least annually and the CCP needs to be update at least quarterly (Coombs, 2019).

Crisis Response

The crisis response is the phase we see most often in the media (traditional and social). The crisis response has both tactical and strategic elements. The tactical elements are about how the crisis response should be delivered. Tactically, a crisis response should be consistent, transparent, and quick. Consistent involves similar messaging coming from the various voices in the organization. This has been called speaking with one voice but that implies one spokesperson and people being overly dependent on the same talking points. You are likely to have multiple people address the crisis in a variety of media. By sharing crisis-related information and discussing the strategies to use in the response, crisis messaging will be consistent. Transparency refers to disclosing information to your stakeholders. Be sure to disclose all information that can affect the stakeholders, especially those related to their physical safety. If you know something that might hurt stakeholders, they need to know that information.

Being quick is the tricky point. How fast is fast? Do you have an hour or do you have 20 minutes to respond? Do not fixate on the exact time of the response. You cannot respond until you have the required information to make a decision. Collecting the necessary information and reviewing it can take time. That is when you can use the pre-drafted holding statements as a quick, initial response then follow-up when you have more information. You do not want days to go by without the organization addressing the crisis. If the worst thing people say about your crisis response is that it was a little slow, you are still doing a great job. Being quick can include the concept of stealing thunder. Stealing thunder is when the organization is the first one to disclose the crisis. This means that when people inside the organization know something has gone wrong, they disclose it before the media or some other entity does. The advantage is that a crisis does less damage to an organization when the organization is the first to disclose the existence of the crisis (Claeys, 2017; Claeys & Cauberghe, 2012). In sports, crises tend to involve misbehavior by people. In many cases the organization (team or league) knows about the problem before anyone else. In those cases, the organization should disclose the information and not wait for it to appear in the media coming from another source. An example would be knowing a player on a team tested positive for performance-enhancing drugs. In stealing thunder, the announcement of the positive test would come from the team and not from the league or some independent testing firm.

Strategy is about the how the information in the response can affect stakeholders' reactions to the crisis and the organization in crisis. Situational crisis communication theory (SCCT) offers advice on crisis communication strategy (Coombs, 2007). SCCT has used research to identify the optimal crisis responses for various types of crises. An optimal crisis response seeks to maximize the benefits to/protection for victims and the organization in crisis. SCCT argues that the optimal crisis response is related to how strongly most stakeholders feel the organization is responsible for the crisis. SCCT holds that in any crisis type, an optimal crisis response begins with the ethical base response. The ethical base response involves seeking to protect people physically from the crisis and to help people cope psychologically with the crisis (Coombs, 2019). Operational crises can create the risk of physical harm to stakeholders. Riots or fire at a sporting event are examples of physically safety threats in the sports context. The crisis managers need to tell people what they need to do to protect themselves physically in a crisis, such as evacuate a facility. Crisis managers help people cope psychologically from a crisis by expressing concern for any victims, showing regret for the actions that caused the crisis, and explaining what is being done to prevent a repeat of the crisis. Given the reputational focus of most sports crises, the psychological aspect is paramount. Notice how teams quickly will release a player for misconduct. Releasing the player is a way to eliminate one source of the problem and prevent a repeat. Releasing the player can provide psychological reassurance to people about the crisis.

For cases when the organization is viewed as very strongly responsible for the crisis, SCCT recommends adding an accepting responsibility and/or compensation to the ethical base response (Coombs, 2019). The organization accepts responsibility by being accountable for the crisis. Even if it was a player, the organization must be accountable for at least part of the crisis. People respect an organization for accepting responsibility. Compensation is when the organization provides financial and/or other benefits (e.g., tickets or merchandise) to victims. An example might be a crisis where the team's web site collapsed during a special ticket release. The web site collapse does interrupt operations and can impact both social evaluations of the team and its revenue. You will have angry fans that had waited hours only to not get a chance to buy tickets. Angry fans can say negative things about the teams to others (both in person and online) and may decide to not buy any other tickets from the team. Anger motivates people to act against the organizations that caused the anger (Coombs & Holladay, 2007). You could compensate those fans with other tickets or some free team merchandise. The compensation is recognition of their pain and suffering. The apology and compensation extend upon the concern for victims begun with the ethical base response. Remember, the crisis should be about the victims and their pain, not the effects of the crisis in the organization (Jackson & Peters, n.d.).

Suboptimal responses as less effective because they do not address the concerns of the victims or potential victims of the crisis. Suboptimal strategies include saying nothing about the crisis or just releasing basic information about the crisis (Claeys & Coombs, 2020). Denial is the worst possible suboptimal strategy because it will make the crisis worse for all involved. Victims and other stakeholders will become angrier and the organization will suffer more damage from the crisis (Coombs, Holladay, & Claeys, 2016). In a crisis, something bad really did happen and the organization does bear some responsibility for the situation. Denial claims no responsibility for the event. Stakeholders become angry because the organization refuses to be accountable for the situation and take the steps necessary to help those affected by the crisis. Consider how BP began its response to the Deepwater Horizon crisis by talking about the cost of the crisis for BP and not about the effects of the oil spill on people living along the Gulf Coast. BP provided a suboptimal response at first in part because it lacked accountability for its actions. You can actually use denial effectively in a paracrisis by explain why your actions are appropriate. In an actual crisis, an organization has some responsibility for the situation making denial a dangerous choice for a crisis response. Stakeholders are unlikely to agree with the denial and that the organization is not at all responsible. Stakeholders are more likely to increase their anger and negative reactions to the organization in crisis when denial is utilized.

Post-Crisis

Post-crisis is when the immediate effects of the crisis are becoming less noticeable. The crisis is no longer the central focus for the organization. There are still communication concerns during this time including follow-up information, remembering, and learning. Stakeholders might need updates or other follow-up information about how the crisis has affected operations. Consider how the NBA provided additional information after creating its bubble to finish their season during the pandemic. Remembering is a way to grieve and to honor for those seriously injured or killed by a crisis. Many professional and college teams have had transportation mishaps that have killed or seriously injured people on or affiliated with the team. Some teams have had crisis where fans were killed or serious injured at events. The victims should be remembered as part of the healing process. Remembering can be some combination of a memorial event and physical memorial. Texas A&M University has a memorial on campus dedicated to the 12 students killed in the 1999 bonfire collapse and holds an event on campus each year on the anniversary of the event. The bonfire was related to fan support for the football team linking the crisis to sports (Tachkova, 2020).

Learning is actually the tricky part of the crisis process. Research has found the organizations are very bad about learning from crises. Often the organization just wants to get past the crisis and forget about the event. People in the organization resist efforts to analyze the crisis and the crisis response for fear of being blamed for anything that went wrong (Smith & Elliot, 2007). Organizations can learn a lot from failures such as crises. The key is finding ways to understand the crisis and the crisis response without creating fear that the results will be used against people. Organizations benefit when they understand what caused a crisis and what was done well or poorly in the crisis response. Understanding the cause of the crisis can help to prevent future crises or to identify a crisis more quickly. Reviewing what was done well or poorly in the crisis response can help to improve the next crisis response by providing more training on what was done poorly and reinforcing what was done well.

Unique Crisis Context for Sport

Sport creates some unique demands on crisis communication that differ from other industries. We have already noted how sport crises are less operational and more reputational in the damage created. What this suggests is that paracrises are common in sports because paracrises are driven by reputational concerns (risks that threaten organizational reputations) (Coombs & Holladay, 2012). Media attention is critical in paracrises because it is the risk of negative publicity and social media comments that amplifies a reputational risk. Teams and athletes are magnets for media attention thereby creating a fertile environment for paracrises (Coombs, 2018). Because of the media attention given to race in the spring of 2020, Cleveland's Major League Baseball team suddenly announced a rethinking of its name ("Indians"). Cleveland's team and mascot had long been a concern with its racist portrayal of Native Americans. In this case, just the thought the team might enter the national media discussion of race was enough to prompt action on the paracrisis. The media attention creates awareness of the risk that, in turn, can damage reputations by changing how stakeholders feel about the organization. The unique context of sports for crisis communication includes fans, sponsors, and levels of crisis.

Fans

As noted in Chapter 3, fans support their teams because they identify with the team and with other fans. Fan identification is a strong bond that is difficult to damage even during a crisis. Research has shown that fans show little change in how they view the organization (social evaluations such as reputation) during a crisis. Furthermore, the fans are more likely to show support rather than feel negative effects from a crisis (Harker, 2019; Zavyalova, Pfarrer, Reger, & Hubbard, 2016). The data indicate that stakeholders who strongly identify with an organization dismiss the negatives crises can create. Fans create the very strong identification making crises less of a threat in sports. Moreover, fans will actively support and defend a sports team during a crisis. Fans will go on social media to defend a team in crisis and attack critics of the team in crisis (Brown & Billings, 2013). Frandsen and Johansen (2017) note that many actors can become crisis communicators during a crisis, not just the organization in crisis. This is known as the multi-vocal approach to crisis communication. These other voices can help the organization in crisis by supporting the crisis communication efforts or hurt the organization by adding additional negative comments to the crisis situation (Frandsen & Johansen, 2010). Not only are fans rather crisis resistant, they also supply support during a crisis.

Keep in mind there is a limit to fan support during a crisis. When there are multiple crises, even fans begin to feel the negative effects of the crisis and decrease support for the organization in crisis (Zayalova et al., 2016). This finding is consistent with SCCT's findings related to repeated crises. SCCT finds that when an organization has a series of crises, stakeholders increase their perceptions that the organization is responsible for the crisis. Increased perceptions of crisis responsibility translates into greater reputational damage for the organization in crisis (Coombs, 1995). Fans are an asset in a sports crisis but fans can be pushed too far—there are limits to the positive crisis effects of stronger identification.

Sponsors

As discussed in Chapter 2, sponsors contribute greatly to the financial resources of teams and even individual athletes. The negative effects of a sports crisis hinge greatly on sponsors. If sponsors still support the athlete or team, the crisis does minimal financial damage. When Maria Sharapova was suspended from tennis for taking a banned drug, many of her sponsors stayed with her mitigating the negative financial effects of the crisis. When NFL player Adrian Peterson was charged with child abuse, he lost all of his contracts. Like fans, sponsor support can lessen the negative effects of a crisis. Sponsors have a unique role to play when powerful leagues have crises. By powerful leagues we mean leagues with strong fan followings, massive broadcast contracts, and lucrative sponsorship deals. The NFL and FIFA are two of the most powerful leagues and are monopolies. People want their product and really have no other source for that product. FIFA had a corruption scandal that lasted for years. For other organizations, this would have been a serious crisis. FIFA largely ignored the corruption problem because it had no effect on its revenue sources. That was until some major sponsors told FIFA to address the problem or lose their support (Fortunato, 2017). Only then did FIFA address the corruption crisis. For powerful leagues, sponsors seem to be the ones to define whether or not the league has a crisis.

Taken together, fans and sponsors can insult those involved in sports crises. When fans and sponsors support a sports entity in crisis, there is little motivation for that entity to manage the crisis. Athletes, teams, and leagues might feel there is no need to communicate much about a crisis and would not be concerned about violating tactical or strategic advice about crisis communication. The context created by fans and sponsors are unique. Sports crisis managers must carefully monitor the reactions of fans and sponsors. If the support of either stakeholder begins to fade, the crisis will become much more serious and damaging.

Levels of Crisis

The levels of crisis are the final unique context for sports crises (Harker, 2018). It should be clear by now that in sports a crisis can involve an athlete, a team, and/or a league. Consider the case of Ray Rice, the former NFL player involved in a domestic violence case. When the video of Ray Rice hitting a woman entered the traditional and social media, the domestic violence case became a crisis for the NFL, not just for the Ravens (Rice's former team), and Rice himself. In crisis management there is a concept known as spillover. Spillover means a crisis can affected other brands within an organization or other organizations within the same industry. A good example is when there is a food recall for produce like spinach. Many consumers stop buying all brands of spinach, not just the one being recalled. The recalled spinach of just one producer will affect sales for the entire industry. Multiple levels can mean multiple crisis managers. As noted in rhetorical arena theory, those multiple voices might work with or against one another. Teams must be concerned that an ARC could become a team crisis if people begin to think the problem is related to policies and practices of the team. Or an ARC might be viewed as a result of the league's culture and the behavior promoted by that culture. For instance, the Ray Rice case highlighted how the NFL had ignored and even suppressed problems with domestic violence among its players for decades (Coombs & Holladay, 2020). Sports crisis managers' teams and leagues must monitor ARCs to determine if the ARC remains localized to the athlete or spreads to the team and/or league. Teams and leagues will have a role to play in ARCs, which is why the NFL commissioner is involved with so many ARCs in the NFL (e.g., Harker, 2018).

Effects of the Sport Context on Crisis Communication

The sports context does have implications for crisis communication during the pre-crisis and response phases. Sports strategic communication is a heavy user of social media and that creates risks. Because of the strong likelihood of paracrises and problems arising in social media, social media listening is critical as part of crisis monitoring in sports. Crisis managers must monitor their own social media as well as being produced by fans. If you are a team, you need to monitor the social media of your personnel and the league for possible warning signs. Social media listening will also alert you to any spillover that is being created by an ACR. The challenge with social media listening as crisis monitoring is understanding when something is noise or a risk that warrants your attention.

As noted earlier, sports actors (leagues, teams, and individuals) sometimes react differently than other entities in crisis. Often sports actors will use suboptimal strategies in crisis communication. This creates problems because the crisis response is less effective because the suboptimal responses do little to protect the organization or stakeholders. Leagues and even teams might feel like they are insulated from the effects of a crisis due to their prominence and fan support. The NFL being slow to address the domestic violence crisis with players and FIFA being incredibly slow to address its corruption crisis are examples of how sports actors can provide suboptimal response because they feel immune from the effects of a crisis. Athletes frequently use denial even though denial does more harm than good if the person is really guilty. Athletes use denial because a crisis can end their careers and source of income. Floyd Landis denied he engaged in blood doping helping him win the Tour de France while Marion Jones denied using performance-enhancing drugs during her track and field efforts. Both athletes faced positive blood tests for banned substances and both eventually plead guilty. However, denial was a logical choice for each because it was the only way to potentially protect their careers. The unique context of sport can result in crisis managers choosing suboptimal crisis responses.

But, as noted earlier, fans provide an upside to the sports context for crisis communication through their supportive behavior. This includes fans flocking to social media and posting messages that support the organization and defend it against the crisis critics. In other industries, crises will damage reputations and organizations have to use optimal crisis response as part of an effort to counter the reputational and financial damage from a crisis (Coombs, 2019). Fans will help organizations by supply positive messages designed to reinforce identification with the organization. By reinforcing identification, the fans help to bolster the crisis-threatened reputation. By supporting a sports actor in crisis, fans make the crisis communication effort a little easier by limiting damage from the crisis and facilitating recovery from the crisis.

Conclusion

As a strategic communicator in sport, you spend a lot of time trying to attract attention and facilitating engagement with your stakeholders. A crisis will make you the center of attention, but in a bad way. One of the biggest mistakes you can make in a crisis is to ghost your stakeholders by going silent. Strategic communicators must communicate even when the situation is painful and difficult—a crisis. Why should your stakeholders respect you and maintain the relationship if you are only there in the good times and not the bad times? In this chapter we have provided the basic information you need to not only be there in bad times but help your stakeholders and organization navigate those bad times and return to good times. The key is understanding optimal crisis responses and how crisis communication can benefit stakeholders and the organization in crisis. Moreover, we have highlighted the areas where sport creates a unique context for crisis communication. The sports context creates some assets and some liabilities for crisis communication. Understanding the unique aspects of the sports context will allow you to be a better crisis manager. This includes managing actual crises and paracrises. Remember, a crisis is not a matter of if but a matter of when making crisis communication a valuable skill for any strategic communicator.

References

Antonetti, P., & Maklan, S. (2016). An extended model of moral outrage at corporate social irresponsibility. *Journal of Business Ethics*, *135*(3), 429–444.

Barton, L. (2001). *Crisis in organizations II* (2nd ed.). Cincinnati, OH: College Divisions South-Western.

Baskin, O., & Aronoff, C. (1988). *Public relations: The profession and the practice* (2nd ed.). Dubuque, IA: William C. Brown.

Brown, N. A., & Billings, A. C. (2013). Sports fans as crisis communicators on social media websites. *Public Relations Review, 39*(1), 74–81.

Bundy, J., Pfarrer, M. D., Short, C. E., & Coombs, W. T. (2017). Crises and crisis management: Integration, interpretation, and research development. *Journal of Management, 43*(6), 1661–1692.

Chen, F. (2019). *Understanding paracrisis communication: Towards developing a framework of paracrisis typology and organizational response strategies* [Doctoral dissertation, Texas A&M University]. TAMU Campus Repository. https://oaktrust.library.tamu.edu/handle/1969.1/186574

Claeys, A. S. (2017). Better safe than sorry: Why organizations in crisis should never hesitate to steal thunder. *Business Horizons, 60*(3), 305–311.

Claeys, A. S., & Cauberghe, V. (2012). Crisis response and crisis timing strategies, two sides of the same coin. *Public Relations Review, 38*(1), 83–88.

Claeys, A. S., & Coombs, W. T. (2020). Organizational crisis communication: Suboptimal crisis response selection decisions and behavioral economics. *Communication Theory, 30*(3), 290–309.

Coombs, W. T. (1995). Choosing the right words: The development of guidelines for the selection of the "appropriate" crisis-response strategies. *Management Communication Quarterly, 8*(4), 447–476.

Coombs, W. T. (2007). Attribution theory as a guide for post-crisis communication research. *Public Relations Review, 33*(2), 135–139.

Coombs, W. T. (2018). Athlete reputational crises: One point for linking situational crisis communication theory and sports crises. In A. C. Billings, W. T. Coombs, & K. A. Brown (Eds.), *Reputational challenges in sport: Theory and application* (pp. 13–25). New York: Routledge.

Coombs, W. T. (2019). *Ongoing crisis communication: Planning, managing, and responding.* London: Sage Publications.

Coombs, W. T., & Holladay, S. J. (2007). The negative communication dynamic: Exploring the impact of stakeholder affect on behavioral intentions. *Journal of Communication management, 11*(4), 300–312.

Coombs, W. T., & Holladay, J. S. (2012). The paracrisis: The challenges created by publicly managing crisis prevention. *Public Relations Review, 38*(3), 408–415.

Coombs, W. T., & Holladay, S.J. (2020). How scandal varies by industry: The effects of industry culture on scandalization of behaviors. In A. Haller & H. Michael (Eds.), *Scandalogy 2* (pp. 144–161). Köln: Herbet Von Halem Verlag.

Coombs, W. T., Holladay, S. J., & Claeys, A. S. (2016). Debunking the myth of denial's effectiveness in crisis communication: Context matters. *Journal of Communication Management, 20*(4), 381–395.

Coombs, W. T., Holladay, S. J., & White, R. (2021). Corporate crises: Sticky crises and corporations. In Y. Jin, B. H. Reber, and G. J Nowak (Eds.), *Advancing crisis communication effectiveness: Integrating public relations scholarship with practice* (pp. 35–51). New York: Routledge.

Coombs, W. T., & Tachkova, E. R. (2019). Scansis as a unique crisis type: Theoretical and practical implications. *Journal of Communication Management. 23*(1), 72–88.

Davies, G., Chun, R., da Silva, R. V., & Roper, S. (2003). *Corporate reputation and competitiveness.* New York: Routledge.

Fortunato, J. A. (2017). The FIFA crisis: Examining sponsor response options. *Journal of Contingencies and Crisis Management, 25*(2), 68–78.

Frandsen, F., & Johansen, W. (2010). Apologizing in a globalizing world: Crisis communication and apologetic ethics. *Corporate Communications, 15*(4), 350–364.

Frandsen, F., & Johansen, W. (2017). *Organizational crisis communication*. Thousand Oaks, CA: Sage.

Harker, J. L. (2018). *Crisis Perceptions, Fan Behaviors, and Egocentric Discussion Networks: An Investigation Into the Impervious Nature of NFL Crises* (Doctoral dissertation, The University of North Carolina at Chapel Hill).

Harker, J. L., (2018). Knee-jerk policymaking in crisis response: A fumbled play by the NFL. In A.C. Billings, W.T. Coombs, & K.A. Brown (Eds.), *Reputational challenges in sport: Theory and application* (pp. 87–103). New York: Routledge.

Harker, J. L. (2019). Identification and crisis: An exploration into the influence of sports identification on stakeholder perceptions of sports-related crisis. *Journal of Sports Media 14*(1), 171–199. https://www.muse.jhu.edu/article/735262.

Heath, R. L. (2010). Crisis communication: Defining the beast and de-marginalizing key publics. In W.T. Coombs, & S. Holladay (Eds.), *The handbook of crisis communication* (pp. 1–13). Malden, MA: Wiley-Blackwell.

Jackson, P. & Peters, R. (n.d.). Issue anticipation/crisis management for beginning professionals. Retrieved from: http://patrickjacksonpr.com/Theories%20 &%20Models/Issues%20Anticipation-Crisis%20Management%20For%20 Beginning%20Professionals%20for%20PRSSA.pdf

Koerber, D., & Zabara, N. (2017). Preventing damage: The psychology of crisis communication buffers in organized sports. *Public Relations Review, 43*(1), 193–200.

Sato, S., Ko, Y. J., Park, C., & Tao, W. (2015). Athlete reputational crisis and consumer evaluation. *European Sport Management Quarterly, 15*(4), 434–453.

Smith, D., & Elliott, D. (2007). Exploring the barriers to learning from crisis: Organizational learning and crisis. *Management Learning, 38*(5), 519–538.

Tachkova, E. R. (2020). Enhancing post-crisis communication through memorials: The case of the bonfire crisis at Texas A&M. *Corporate Communications: An International Journal. 25*(3), 395–411.

Zavyalova, A., Pfarrer, M. D., Reger, R. K., & Hubbard, T. D. (2016). Reputation as a benefit and a burden? How stakeholders' organizational identification affects the role of reputation following a negative event. *Academy of Management Journal, 59*(1), 253–276.

Index

Note: Page numbers in **bold** refer to figures, page numbers in *italic* refer to tables